PRAISE FOR THE UNL

"...this book...captures the true essence of life struggles...an unpredicted reading. [I'll] use these lessons for rest of my journey..."

"This is one of the best books I have ever read...it can help with your life regardless of where you're at."

"Powerful book...like having a shot of whiskey to the soul!"

"this is the most accessible, no-holds-barred handbook to guide you through [limiting beliefs]"

"WOW, what an amazing work this is! I am still in tears, fabulous read!"

"This is the best book on changing your life..."

"If you feel stuck, this is the book to read..."

"Get your pen and paper handy...time to get real. Easy quick read...Just buy it!"

"...Don't second guess reading this book!"

"It made me happier - amazing how can one book change one's perspective!"

"[this book] made a noticeable difference in my life already and it's only been a few days."

"I have read a lot of self-help books but this is one of the most life changing books I have read."

A MUST READ! ...packed with a wealth of information. It's made its way as one of my favorites!"

"This read was one of the best I have had in a long while."

"Great, quick read that will surely leave you in a better place than when you began."

"Motivational, realistic and to the point...the author drops power bombs..."

"Life Changing. This book has really helped...I plan on rereading this book."

THE
UNLIMITED
SELF

JONATHAN

HESTON

The Unlimited Self: Destroy Limiting Beliefs, Uncover Inner Greatness, and Live the Good Life.

Copyright © 2015 by Jonathan Heston

Jonathan Heston
jonathan@theinnerarena.com
http://www.theunlimitedself.net

Front Cover Design by Jonathan Heston

ISBN-13: 978-1535274319

Library of Congress Control Number:

First Printed Edition

The Unlimited Self is not meant as a substitute for counseling. The author is not dispensing medical or psychological advice. Whenever there is concern about physical or emotional illness, a qualified professional should be consulted. The author shall have neither liability or responsibility to any person or entity with respect to any loss, damage, injury, ailment, caused or alleged to be caused directly or indirectly by the information or lack of information in this book.

for Chloe

| THE UNLIMITED SELF

A loud THANK YOU to all readers who supported the
Kindle edition! This print edition was made
possible because of your enthusiasm,
recommendations, and support!

CONTENTS

STEP 1: FEEDING

HOW LIMITING BELIEFS ARE KEPT ALIVE & WELL

STEP 2: READYING

RECONTEXTUALIZE THE WORLD FOR YOUR POWER

STEP 3: EXPOSING

HACKING METHODS USEFUL FOR THE OBLITERATION OF

LIMITING BELIEFS

———————

STEP 4: EMERGING

ON THE FINDING & GIVING OF YOUR GREATEST GIFT

———————

IS THIS BOOK FOR YOU?

Not sure if having a passionate "unlimited" life, moving into your greatness, and giving your deepest gift to the world is really for you? Here are some burning doubts many have before they begin their journey toward freedom...

Do I have to know what my passion is or have huge dreams of greatness?

Nope. Greatness isn't a destination; it's a process. Anything outside your current reach and capacity is greatness. All you get to do is take the next step. Many people have no clue what they want or what their passion is. That's ok. This book will help you move as far down the path as you wish to go. But I'll warn you...this path can be addictive. I have a feeling, once you taste true expansion, you'll want more.

Do I have to be a young twenty-something with nothing to hold me back?

No. Anyone can discover a more fulfilling path. This has nothing to do with age or responsibility and has everything to do with identifying and unlearning the beliefs that don't help or empower you to be your authentic self. The idea that something is holding you back is a limiting belief in your abilities and greatness.

What if I'm already doing something I'm passionate about, and getting paid nicely for it?

Then these tools are even more important. The achievement of success has tricky ways of sabotaging and undermining our quality of life...from loneliness, to moments of wanting to burn it all to the ground, to becoming addicted to the hustle and grind. Pursuing your greatness is amazing, but doing it on a poor foundation can be a recipe for long-term disaster. This book will help build a strong foundation and keep you creating and expanding in a powerful way, instead of yo-yoing between an addiction to the hustle and a full-blown desire to walk from it all. So yes. Keep reading.

What if I'm content with my job, career, relationships, and life?

If you're not expanding, you're dying. Are you going to settle for a 'content' life, instead of a fantastic life? Stagnation, boredom, and the cult of comfort are some of the most real and dangerous threats to fulfillment, significance, and happiness, especially as life moves forward. I'd encourage you to keep reading.

STOP!

DON'T FORGET YOUR BONUSES

Four powerful resources come with this book.

1. If you're an entrepreneur or business owner who has already built a measure of success, and you still have a deep internal drive to keep expanding, then you probably experience the "entrepreneurial rollercoaster" – where Friday you feel on top of the world, and Tuesday you're in the pits. What if you could eliminate the valleys and have <u>consistent</u> access to your personal power? This Masterclass covers my **Power Pyramid System** – the framework my clients use to eliminate the "drops" in their emotional rollercoaster so they can pull off their scariest dreams, critical priorities and greatest life. And don't worry, it's a stand-alone training with new content, not a repeat of what I teach in this book.

2. Maybe you're not sure how to find your full voice and passion? I'll give you my **Passion and Purpose Guide** for free, that will get you started in under 10 minutes.

3. Information, without action, leaves you hanging. So, I created an action plan you can use to integrate these principles into your OWN Unlimited Self life. My guide, **THE MAP**, will show you the path to turn this information into practical application.

4. Relationships and community are key, so I'm giving you access to my **Facebook Tribe** filled with like-minded people, discussion, and more of my musings and trainings.

To get all 4 of these bonuses...just go here, stick in your name and email address, and you'll have them instantly!
http://www.theunlimitedself.net/bb/

FOREWORD

Walking the path toward the unlimited life is crazy. To succeed, you have to stand firm in the face of opposition. You have to trust yourself. And you have to do it while every fear, doubt, and limiting belief is exposed. You're forced to face every inner demon you've spent your life hiding from.

Because of this discomfort, many people turn back and never experience true freedom. Yet, others have a desire that burns big enough to sustain their journey for greatness through every up and down.

What lit your flame of desire for a truly unlimited life? For me, books were the spark.

I'll never forget reading 'Rich Dad, Poor Dad' and feeling a blaze of excitement. I quickly announced to my family I would make passive income, so I wouldn't have to work anymore. They just looked at me in utter confusion and doubt. But I did it.

Now, as I help hundreds of entrepreneurs start businesses, the single greatest tool needed isn't tactics, strategies, or systems. It's the reversing of limiting beliefs.

Maybe you know you are meant for something more, but have no clue how to get there. Maybe you're looking for your flame to be lit.

If so, I hope this book is your spark. I hope, as you walk with Jonathan deep into the world of unlocking limiting beliefs, you too will awaken to a new reality of wholeness.

When I first met Jonathan, he was frustrated and searching, feeling stuck in a 9-5 job he hated, and habits and mindsets he knew were massively limiting his potential.

Since then, he has intentionally faced and tackled many limiting beliefs. He's stopped making excuses about being "stuck" and, finally, made the leap out of his comfort zone toward doing what he'd only dreamed of doing before. And he's made the major step toward living his purpose by gifting us with this guide to working through inner limitations.

Jonathan lives the message of this book. I'd encourage you to take full advantage of this dude's wisdom, so you too can be empowered to live the unlimited life.

Dane Maxwell
Founder of The Foundation
November 25, 2014

PREFACE

A

PERSONAL

CONFESSION

Those pressing into greatness give before they are ready. They put themselves out to the world before they're perfect, before it's comfortable, and before having it all figured out.

This book is me doing just that. It's scary. Even though I've lived what I'm writing, and I've seen the fulfillment in my own life, I'm not some rich happiness guru.

Let me be vulnerable with you. I don't yet have many of the "typical" external trappings that many would associate with success...

I have zero financial assets to my name. My wife, Chloe, and I sometimes have trouble deeply connecting. My daughter, Shiloh (three years old), is continually challenging us beyond our comfort zones. I have a herniated disc in my back, I'm bald, and slightly overweight. We chose to drive a Toyota Camry to 475,000 miles, and our current Camry has recently had transmission problems (it has nearly 200,000 miles). I'm a newbie with my "money conscience." I need to invoice a client for several thousand, and I've been putting it off the last two days. I don't always love every minute of my day...sometimes, I have days when I question everything and deeply doubt myself. Right now, my spiritual walk is like riding a roller coaster in the dark. Some weeks, I'm so unbalanced and overcommitted I leave my family out to dry, while I work for eighty hours. Did I mention I start things, without seeing them through to completion?

Being vulnerable and honest with you about where I am is the best thing I can do for myself, and for you, because the journey of self-evolution starts with admitting where you are.

If my thoughts help one person truly achieve their inner greatness, that will be enough to make this book worth it.

On my short journey, I've been blessed with multiple perspectives, tools, and hacks that have allowed me to step out of my comfort zone, embrace my fear, love others (and myself), and live in my full potential. I've leaned into it. Invested in it. Sought it out. I've walked away from countless opportunities I knew I would feel trapped in, because they didn't align with the greater gift I can give to the world.

I proposed to Chloe after one week of dating. I toured the United States for two years playing music I love. I quickly rose in the ranks of multiple jobs (even though I didn't enjoy them), creating systems that helped everything run with greater success. In the middle of working these eighty hour weeks, I taught myself specific skills, so I wouldn't be stuck in a J-O-B forever. The last few years, I've spent nearly half my annual income on business and personal growth. I quit my good 9-5 job, before I had a clear plan set in place, so I could live in alignment with who I am. I've developed the skills and expertise to help men enter their own Inner Arena and share their greatness with the world.

But most importantly...I didn't give up on myself. I've learned to accept myself (even after years of failing hard), and I've continued to tenaciously press forward to be the best person I can be.

In a few years, I may look back and chuckle at some of what I will share in this book. Because I'll keep growing. But that's part of the point. Life is never stagnant. It's always evolving.

So from one peer on a journey to a fellow traveler of life...
Let's evolve together.

— Jonathan Heston
Fall of 2014

P.S. I finished this book over a year ago, and it sat on my computer as other things occupied my energy. I have left the book as is (besides my "about the author" page). Enjoy.

— Jonathan Heston, Fall of 2015
Founder of The Unlimited Self Movement and The Power Pyramid System.

www.theunlimitedself.net

INTRODUCTION

JOURNEY

TO

THE

EDGE

OF

GREATNESS

| THE UNLIMITED SELF

What lies behind us and what lies before us are tiny matters compared to what lies within us.

R A L P H   W A L D O   E M E R S O N

Most people die at twenty-five and aren't buried until they're seventy-five.

B E N J A M I N   F R A N K L I N

Join me as we step to the edge of a precipice...heart rate jacked...breath shallow and jerky...gut tightened.

Our toes reach just over the edge. We raise our eyes to the expanse, despite the violent wind of our fears threatening to pull us over into the chasm. We extend our arms—unabashedly—and open ourselves to the thrill.

And then...we reach the moment of exhilarating freedom, where fear disappears and wild faith surges. Where the glory of life reveals itself. Where we know, with all certainty, even death itself would have been worth this.

Welcome to the Edge, where your burning desire to be great drives you to face and conquer deep limiting beliefs, push past comfort zones, and offer your authentic self to the world.

The Edge looks different for everyone. It might look like quitting your job, confessing a blunder to a loved one, or trying to transform your health. It might be as complex as learning to dance through life in a committed relationship or as simple as making a set of phone calls to explode your opportunity. Maybe, for you, it's speaking in front of people, doing something your friends and family think is crazy, forgiving someone for a deep hurt, or moving your net worth from five million to ten million.

Whatever your Edge of greatness is, it will be uncomfortable.

That's why so many stay far away from their Edge. They may often imagine "taking the step", imagining how frightening it would be, while longing for the thrill of triumph. Yet, they play it safe. Fifty feet from the edge. They may wonder what the view is like, debating and theorizing with others about it. They may try to convince themselves they're not missing out, while admiring from a distance those who have stepped up to their own Edge. They may even make plans to walk to their Edge, spending days brainstorming detailed strategies and stocking up on "needed" supplies.

Then, despite all the dreaming and planning...at the end of it all...they lie on their deathbed, filled with deep regret they never stepped up all the way.

It's a travesty how many people have fallen prey to apathy. Their numbers are only growing. I call those in this group Apathetics.

How do people become this? What holds Apathetics back from living great lives? When we search for the hidden variables, we find they all point back to one thing: limiting beliefs.

Do you ever notice your limiting beliefs? They're what prevent you from stepping up to your Edge. They're what keep you dreaming, but never doing. They're what keep you doubting, worrying, stressing, feeling small and weak, stuck, procrastinating, unfulfilled, and unhappy. And slowly...as life speeds by...there's that claustrophobic grip that keeps tightening around your heart.

If you want to leave the crowd of Apathetics for good, understand t the quality of your life, work, relationships, spiritual walk, and health all have one thing in common...you.

The key to experiencing life without limits is upgrading you. This "game" of upgrading you is what I call the Inner Arena. When you enter your Inner Arena, you become an Edge Walker. You begin intentionally facing and fighting the deep fears and beliefs that have kept you locked up for too long, so you can walk to your Edge and experience the thrill of living life free of limits and true to yourself.

Focusing on the Inner Arena helps you avoid the all-too-common success trap, where you have a good career, yet are unfulfilled. Or you're a great parent, but don't have abundant finances or health. This trap results from embracing strategy and tactics in specific areas, while ignoring your Inner Arena, the game going on deep under the surface. Sustained, this approach leads to burnout and a deep sense of not being fulfilled. Sure, rocking it in one area might feel great for a while, but look at the writing on the wall...it will never take you where you long to be.

Edge Walkers understand it all comes down to upgrading themselves. This is the reason limiting beliefs are not to be skimmed over. You can learn to stand at your Edge in every area of your life by intentionally hacking limiting beliefs. The only thing holding you back from where you are and where you want to be are the perceptions you hold about yourself, others, and reality. These perceptions cut you off from authentic love, success, and fulfillment. Identifying and changing these perceptions and beliefs is the fast track to freedom, because it transforms you. When transformed, everything you touch is transformed.

If you're tired of going in circles and are ready to live a life of no regrets...then this book was written for you. I've written it, hoping to supply the inspiration and help you need to finally walk to your Edge and live there.

Join me on a lightening-speed journey, where soon you will have your own ninja-hacking skills. Let's search for and find the place where you are fully alive, affecting the world with your gift, and being the great person you were ... where success comes effortlessly, and you are blown away by how rich and fulfilling each day is.

EDGE WALKERS VS. APATHETICS

The difference between Edge Walkers, who enter their Inner Arena, and Apathetics can be dangerously subtle. Perhaps, seeing the difference may give you the push you need to join the great legion of Edge Walkers.

Apathetics: Are driven by their desire to be comfortable.
Edge Walkers: Know that true fulfillment is found at their Edge. They are driven by the desire to make their own and other's lives richer.

Apathetics: Constantly battle internal stress and negativity. They feel stuck as this battle continues year after year.
Edge Walkers: Realize everything they experience flows out of one thing: themselves. They address the stress and negativity at its source.

Apathetics: Rely on other's perceptions to dictate their ultimate self-worth. They worry about what others think of them, more than they care to admit.
Edge Walkers: Value and nurture their self-worth and refuse to give anyone else power or control over it.

Apathetics: Link their happiness to external circumstances or internal perfection. "I will be fulfilled when..."

Edge Walkers: Know happiness comes from a choice within themselves, so they focus on nourishing their internal world.

Apathetics: Believe their thoughts are a full expression of their identity. These thoughts are likely unexamined.
Edge Walkers: Recognize their thoughts are conversations, separate from their identity. They learn to process and let go of thoughts not helping them.

Apathetics: Assume their perception of reality is "true", and they unquestioningly filter information through these preconceived ideas.
Edge Walkers: Examine how their perceptions are affecting their goals. They have an open mind and a willingness to consider new perceptions that would better serve them.

Apathetics: Spend most of their thought and emotional energy on what others should or should not be doing, and on what should or should not have happened.
Edge Walkers: Spend most of their thought and energy on embracing reality. They nurture love and appreciation within themselves, and these are the lenses through which they view others.

Apathetics: Wait for something external to "fire up" their dream of a different life. They get stuck in preparation, perfectionism, and excuses.
Edge Walkers: Volunteer their greatest gifts to the world consistently, waiting for nothing, not even themselves.

What are your gut feelings as you read through this list? Do you feel the Apathetic descriptions ringing truer in your life than those of the Edge Walker? If so, that's actually awesome! It bears repeating; reality is the best starting place for moving forward.

If you are seeing areas where you are not happy with yourself or your life, then you are ready for the next step...to create the life you've always wanted.

Things can only get better from here. And, trust me, things can get good.

HOW TO USE THIS BOOK

Learning how to exchange a mediocre life for an unlimited life of freedom need not be obscure or complicated. I've broken it down into four simple steps. Each step builds on the one before it, so unlike most books, it is important you read in order, especially if you haven't previously worked with limiting beliefs.

I also recommend you read through Steps 1 and 2 slowly, with a pen and paper in hand. Jot down any limiting beliefs that come to mind as you read, so that once you get to Step 3, you will have a list to work through. It is this intentional interaction that will cause the fastest change in your life.

STEP 1: FEEDING

This is an inside look into the dark ways that limiting beliefs are formed: from the confusing stories our minds tell us, to traumatizing events from our childhood, to our preprogrammed responses to emotions. This section will also show us exactly how to identify our personal set of limiting beliefs.

STEP 2: READYING

To work through limiting beliefs, we must start with a new foundation. This section helps build transformational core concepts as a foundation for us to stand on, so we won't feel like we're in quicksand, while implementing the specific tactics in Step 3.

STEP 3: EXPOSING

This is where we dig into the ninja skills. These powerful exercises allow us to deconstruct the specific limiting beliefs holding us back in our journey.

STEP 4: EMERGING

After working through limiting beliefs, life truly becomes extraordinary. This section provides practical and proven wisdom to ensure we live successfully on our Edge.

STEP 1:

FEEDING

HOW

BELIEFS

ARE

KEPT

ALIVE

&

WELL

If you know the enemy and know yourself, you need not fear the result of a hundred battles.

If you know yourself but not the enemy, for every victory gained you will also suffer a defeat.

If you know neither the enemy nor yourself, you will succumb in every battle.

SUN TZU

While limiting beliefs are fairly simple, understanding the picture of where they come from and why we have them is not. That is why we get stuck. We don't understand the context of our thoughts, so we are led to a deepening abyss of confusion and self-doubt.

Maybe some of us have jumped on the motivational bandwagons of "Crush it", "Just do it", "Stay positive", and "Attract good things" (and maybe some of us don't touch the "hype" with a ten-foot pole). Doing whatever it takes, staying positive, and exercising the law of attraction are all great for maintaining in the proper context. But they disconnect us from reality when we're struggling with the real enemy—limiting beliefs. And while we can often push through and feel good for a moment, our emotional high may quickly plummet, causing significant internal dissonance.

We have our positive, work hard, fight-through side of ourselves...and our dark, limited side. If we don't dig deep into the internal causes of our limiting beliefs to understand the underlying process of what is happening, this raging internal war can, eventually, cause so much confusion we give up entirely.

You don't have to fight this ongoing war, once you understand limiting beliefs.

In this Feeding section, we will explore why we are constantly prone to adopting limiting beliefs, instead of powerful beliefs. We'll also look at the intel that enables you to hack limiting beliefs, so you have the proper context for all the feel-good motivational, work hard, self-help stuff.

Once you truly understand the Feeding process, the world will appear different.

Let's dig in.

1.

LIVING
OFF
STORIES

THE
VOICES
KEEPING
YOU
FROM
REALITY

How could they see anything but the shadows if they were

never allowed to move their heads?

PLATO

Our mind is awesome at observing and communicating. It's decent at storing information. But it's weak at discovering truth and making decisions.

Our mind has a core job, and it does it well. It takes in tons of information, organizes all that data, and spits out something, which seemingly makes sense of it all. It connects dots and feeds us a "story" that explains your internal question, negative emotion, or any perceived possibility that:

o   Someone may remove their approval or love from us
o   Someone may disrespect us (especially in front of others)
o   We may lose our safety or security
o   We may experience pain

o   We may experience negative emotions

Feeling sad? Your mind senses the feeling and goes into overdrive, digging through your subconscious, memories, circumstances, thoughts, and your day...and then gives you a nice gift-wrapped package, explaining the cause.

Wondering why something didn't work out? Brain overdrive! Story coming. "You failed here. They thought this. Why didn't you do this?"

But here is the catch. *Your mind is not to be trusted.*

Because our minds are so powerful and refer to ourselves in first person, we think we are our thoughts. We believe our thoughts originate from our identity. So, if we are thinking something shameful, we think we are shameful. If we are thinking something hateful...we think we are hateful. If we are thinking something stupid...we think we are stupid.

This is ridiculous. Remember, our mind's main job is to give us thoughts. Its job is to create plausible scenarios or possibilities. Its job is to make sense of everything happening in our world. And it will use anything from our past, the present, or our imagination as ammo. Our minds have no concept of time. If something was accepted as truth at age three, it may still be accepted as truth at age thirty or ninety.

So, I'm inviting you. Instead of believing your thoughts are your identity, think of them as little bursts of organized energy. Simply think of them as ideas being produced for you to consider, organize, and direct for your benefit.

Look at it this way. Is what you see with your eyes "you"? Of course not. You watch the world, consider the information, and react to what you see. Your eyes are a tool for you, but what they view is not your identity. Your thoughts are much the same. They deliver a perception of information to help you navigate through this world. Unfortunately, we are not taught to live an examined thought life, so we naturally come to believe we are this navigation device and feel what we perceive is 100% true or factual. This causes problems with our self-esteem and with our beliefs about the world, because this navigation device is amazing at giving us poor information.

Imagine living life: getting fed poor information...a construct that connects dots and sounds plausible...a story that makes sense of random emotions...but is not factual or even very useful to grow and mature...and thinking every bit of it was a true representation of who you are at your core.

If your body is functioning at a low level due to lack of sleep and a poor diet, you might feel emotionally discouraged. Your mind, getting these discouragement signals, must find a cause-and-effect scenario. If you are unaware of the link between your diet, sleep, and hormones, your mind might link the cause of your discouragement to your spouse or to your perceived failures as a business owner. If unexamined, you accept this story as truth, and your mind starts finding and connecting more "dots" to support this view of reality, working hard to find past evidence and eagerly waiting to jump on future evidence.

An awesome real-life example of this: A successful entrepreneur was teaching a high-end mastermind class of fifty or so students. These students paid thousands to be there. This man took the stage to massive applause and started dropping knowledge bombs. About three minutes into his one-hour presentation, he noticed a man texting in the front row. He didn't let it get to him. Five minutes later, he noticed the guy was still texting. As the hour ran on, the texting continued, annoying the speaker. It was distracting his energy, and he felt greatly disrespected by this man, who had the audacity to be on his cell phone—right there in the front row! Finally, no longer able to ignore the frustration and resentment building inside, the speaker couldn't help himself and called out the texter, "If you have important business you need to attend to—please be kind enough to conduct it out in the hall and return once you are finished." The texter was very confused. All this time, he had been diligently taking notes on his phone, since his computer had crashed the night before and was unusable. Suddenly, the speaker felt the whip-lash of having accepted his mind's stories as truth, when they were false.

Let's be honest. We're all receiving and accepting stories like this from our minds all day long. This example shows us how powerful our mind games can be with relatively small things. Imagine how warped our perceptions can be when we have accepted and built these stories for years, especially about our own self-worth.

Then we get caught in another trap, "Why am I so negative? Why do I feel like such failure? Why do I care about what other people think?" And the loop goes on and on. The more we accept thoughts, without thinking about them, and the more we define ourselves by what we think, the more likely it is we are living in some internal stress loop of suffering. Belief in our unexamined internal stories is not a belief in facts.

Limiting beliefs are partially the stories our mind feeds us, which limit who we are and where we want to go. They disempower, instead of empower us.

The great news is existing beliefs can be deconstructed and new beliefs fashioned. By hacking limiting beliefs, thoughts can be leveraged for our massive advantage, exponentially increasing freedom and powerful beliefs.

2.

THE SECRET WARNING SYSTEM YOU'VE BEEN TRAINED TO IGNORE

It is not the facts that we fear but our feelings about them.

DAVID HAWKINS

The fastest way to freedom is to feel your feelings.

GITA BELLIN

S tudies show that, beyond the brain in our skulls, we have a second "brain" operating in our bodies. The enteric nervous system houses this other brain, responsible for communicating to our "first brain" about our mental state and those strong feelings in our gut. Some people call this intuition. Some people call it emotions. Regardless of the label, there is a symbiotic and critical relationship between our mind and emotions. They fuel and trigger each other.

Maybe one day, I feel sad (second brain). My mind (first brain), knowing I feel sad, seeks out a story to justify my feeling. Conversely, as I think of something (my first brain at work), my mind's "story" triggers a state of emotion in my body (or the "second brain").

It's a back and forth relationship. It is important to understand this, because in our culture, emotions are distrusted. We've been taught that emotions indicate a lack of self-control.

This creates two groups of dysfunction. In the first group are those who always "shelve" their emotions. They are good at suppressing emotions, to the point of feeling numb. Then there's the other group, who strongly experience and express everything they feel, whether it's anger, frustration, or sadness, at the expense of those around them. Those in this group may also suppress their emotions...but usually, only when they feel guilt after having just gone on an emotional free-for-all. Both groups of people are living in a love/hate relationship with their "second brain", which will cause imbalance in their lives. And both groups are being controlled by their emotions. This control goes back to childhood.

Picture a toddler playing on the floor. This little fellow is upset, because one of his toys has just been taken away. He doesn't know why; he cannot even comprehend why. He simply wants what was removed. The only communication available to this little boy is to cry and throw a fit. What is the likely result? The toddler will be reprimanded, being trained to suppress his emotions, or he may be ignored, being trained to be even more expressive of his emotions in order defy or gain the concern of someone.

When my daughter is processing her emotions, it makes me feel uncomfortable. Often her emotions bleed into my own emotions, because I don't fully understand and suppress my emotions, I have a strong desire to suppress hers as well.

An angry person in a room full of adults easily, even if unconsciously, transfers anger and agitation to the others present.

This is the same for more positive emotions. The energy of an excited and passionate person is also contagious. (Have you ever been to a network marketing conference?)

We rarely know how to be present with others experiencing extreme sadness, anger, or fear. This is because most of us feel guilty when we feel strong or extreme emotions.

By reacting to our emotions through suppression or uncontrolled expression, we are attempting to hide a gaping wound.

And that's the problem.

We can attempt to hide our emotions for a little while, but these feelings, rooted in our childhood, will continue to manifest themselves well into adulthood. If negative emotions keep "popping up" at random times, what type of stories will our minds create? Limiting ones. Each time they show up, our minds will attempt to explain them. Hence, we create a whole new set of limiting beliefs.

Those who have a healthy relationship with their emotions are a rare breed. Most people overly suppress their emotions, are controlled by every whim of their emotions, or fluctuate wildly between the two extremes.

But there is a better way. Instead of viewing emotions as something foreign to be suppressed and ignored...instead of viewing them as something to fear or feel guilty about...instead of viewing them as your identity...Consider this. Emotions are an advanced warning system within the body. They are simply energy in motion. We've just never been trained to use them properly. Emotions simply want to be acknowledged, their warnings noted.

Imagine your emotions as a part of your body, raising their hand (like in a classroom) and saying "Excuse me! I'm a little bit worried about doing that because of XYZ!" Simply recognizing and feeling an emotion that is present, opens us to deeper wisdom.

Emotions are not the enemy, and they are not undesirable. Emotions are a significant barometer of life, designed to give us important feedback about our circumstances and decisions. I'm not saying emotions are always the master. But they supply important data we cannot afford to ignore and suppress.

Once we understand how they are trying to help us, we can use our emotions and subconscious as powerful tools and one of the biggest accelerators of our success. We will take a deep dive into how to leverage this tool in the Exposing section.

3.

THE
REARVIEW
MIRROR
&
VOWS
OF
IGNORANCE

What's past is a prologue.

WILLIAM SHAKESPEARE

We've all been kids and experienced traumatic events in our past. These things from our childhood are stored in the emotions and subconscious, which have no understanding of time. While our conscious memories may forget the drama, our emotions and subconscious continue to carry the feelings created by these events. So when we encounter a similar situation as an adult, our system will often revert to the feelings and fears felt originally.

I don't want us to get stuck on becoming victims of our pasts through excessive inward searching or excuse-making. However, it is important to understand the context of our past experiences, so we have more grace for ourselves and realize it isn't our "fault" we have stuff to process.

PAST EVENTS

Different moments in our lives offered extreme emotions that didn't feel very good. These emotions, triggered in an extreme event, were probably handled in one of three ways.

1. A deep-rooted belief was built (often on stories centered on what other people thought of you, your personal failures, or what you thought of others).

2. A strong inner vow was made to avoid future pain. This was a strong self-promise, made out of deep anger, sadness, guilt, or shame, which led to future suppression of that same emotion.

3. The negative and painful emotions were suppressed (and then continually felt throughout life).

Any of these scenarios will cause limiting beliefs. We've looked at how we suppress our emotions, so let's look at deep-rooted beliefs and inner vows in more depth.

DEEP-ROOTED BELIEFS

It is important to understand these beliefs attached to childhood trauma can feel true. When elaborate stories are built in traumatic moments, they are solidified by outside events, other people, yourself, and your emotions. This makes it a deep-rooted belief, not simply a brain-story you randomly accept. This deeper belief strongly filters your perceptions of yourself, the world throughout your entire life. You've spent a lifetime finding evidence to support the belief and seldom can you just say, "That silly," and let it go, even though others may recognize how irrational it is.

For example, I worked with one woman, who worked hard to prepare awesome meals for her family, but frequently felt defeated and frustrated over her abilities as a cook. She was able to uncover a limiting belief strongly connecting shame to her work in the kitchen. She remembered how, as a young child, she had attempted to make mulberry jam and had stained the kitchen counters. This was met with great disapproval from her mother. The shame she felt as a five-year-old for attempting to create in the kitchen, kept her from feeling fulfilled decades later as she provided meals for her family.

We will take a deep dive into these deep-seated beliefs later, but for now, it's important you recognize some of the "power" behind these unquestioned beliefs.

INNER VOWS

Inner vows are much like deep-rooted beliefs, where you've built an elaborate story, but in addition, you've also made a deep commitment to yourself never to be a certain way or always to be a certain way. "I'll never be fat like my mother." "I'll never let anyone get close to me again." "I'll never be irresponsible like my father." These inner vows greatly limit your life. Their power is rooted in judgment, pain, and negativity, rather than in love and freedom.

I recently heard an example of an inner vow from a friend of mine. This friend had always struggled with eating a healthy diet. Any time he ate healthy, he'd feel a strong need (that went beyond "cravings") for the unhealthy foods he wasn't eating and an aversion to most of the healthy things he wanted to eat. One day, as he was contemplating this, a very clear memory came to his mind. In the memory, he was around four years old. His mom had just told him he couldn't eat a certain treat, and at that moment, feeling a surge of rebellion, this little boy resolved, "When I am grown up, I'm going to eat whatever I want!" This inner vow followed my friend into his adult life, affecting his subconscious mind every time he went to the fridge to get something to eat.

The awesome thing is, once he worked through this memory and the related limiting beliefs, he immediately felt freedom in his diet. Suddenly, he craved raw spinach and carrots. He also felt a deep contentment in his healthy diet choices, and no longer felt like he was missing out on all those "forbidden treats."

Another example of an inner vow would be a child vowing to never be angry, because their parent's anger is so distressing. This will make processing anger challenging throughout the child's life. As an adult, they cannot objectively look at the emotional data of anger, learn from it, and let it go.

We will become more and more like what we have judged and then sworn not to become, because our mind constantly compares our thoughts and emotions to those we've judged. This constant exposure attracts the very same behaviors into our own lives.

Some vows we make as children may seem "good", like "I will never be poor," or "I will always help those in need," or "I will never yell at my family." Even these kinds of vows are made out of judgment, and any decision rooted in judgment will inevitably lead to pain or great unbalance in our lives. Also, these vows are often rooted in our determination to have absolute control over our destiny, which can thwart us from being all that we are meant to be.

There are many ways to locate inner vows. One simple exercise is to ask yourself if you've ever resolved, "I will..." or "I will never..." in response to something you judged in your parents. If you remember having said something like this, consider how fulfilled or successful you have been in that resolution. Do you feel your life is thriving…or are you are constantly struggling and failing…or perhaps, you've succeeded in your resolution, but your relationships have paid a high price for it? Other clues of inner vows are excessive negative emotions, compulsive behavior, extreme responses to any situation, or engrained negative expectations towards others (a man may have judged his mother for being too emotional and then judges all women to be that way and treats them accordingly).

Simply recognizing how inner vows weaken, rather than strengthen, our lives is the first step to redefining these vows to empower you.

We'll explore that process more later.

4.

TRACK
LIMITING
BELIEFS

FIVE

CLUES

TO

UNCOVER

WHAT

YOU

DON'T

KNOW

For what I am doing, I do not understand; for I am not practicing

what I would like to do, but I am doing the very thing I hate.

THE APOSTLE PAUL

L imiting beliefs can surface in every area of your life. Some give
many clues about the root cause, and some are so hidden you
likely cannot find them without a close friend, mentor, or coach
helping you uncover them.

Before you try to find limiting beliefs, you need to recognize
two things.

First, recognize you don't know everything and, therefore,
choose humility. This frees your mind to learn. If you are unwilling to
question your current beliefs, you cannot deconstruct any limiting
beliefs.

Second, remember you are doing your best with what you
have. We'll dig into this more a little later, but for now, don't feel
guilty if you find a whole series of limiting beliefs holding you back.
The more you recognize reality, without wallowing in shame, the

easier it is to move forward. Remember, your beliefs do not determine your worth.

The areas you will find limiting beliefs are as varied as you are: life mission, health, business, relationships, finances, spirituality, sexuality, etc.

Following are five clues to areas where you may have limiting beliefs.

FIRST: YOU FEEL AS IF YOUR POWER IS LIMITED

If at the end of the day, when you are hard-pressed, you know you have better in you, yet for whatever reason, no matter how hard you try, no matter how hard you promise yourself, no matter how hard you work, you just can't grow...if you have any area in your life, where you continually do what you don't want to do...you probably have a limiting belief holding you back.

You might even have a layered set of a few different beliefs limiting you in an area. This "layering" happens over time, when you continually try to break free of a limiting belief, yet fail, causing you to build "reasons" and beliefs for being stuck.

For example, with my health, I have had a hard time letting go of sugar, because of an inner belief like: "Without sugary treats, I won't be happy." Two limiting beliefs are layered in that statement.

1. Sugar is the only thing that can make treats taste delicious.

2. I can only be happy if I'm eating treats with sugar.

...Limiting my power and outlook, right?

When you identify areas where you continually have a struggle, you have found areas where you are likely dealing with a strong limiting belief or set of limiting beliefs.

SECOND: YOU FEEL DEEP FEAR OR DEEP DISCOMFORT

When you live a life on the Edge, and decide to give your greatest gift to the world, you will run into very practical obstacles and need to take action steps, which will feel very uncomfortable. Anyone driven by a deep mission will always face areas of discomfort and stretching. However, a limiting belief will cause what should be a simple stretching of one's comfort zone to be paralyzing uncomfortable.

Before addressing these limiting beliefs, you can go in one of two directions. Either you can dive into the discomfort or retreat.

Retreat has many faces: taking a less efficient path, procrastinating, busy work, giving up on your dreams, taking a "course" that will make you feel more comfortable...

Whatever path of retreat you take, know you're just postponing facing your growth and trading the discomfort of success for the discomfort of regret.

That's why deconstructing limiting beliefs is so empowering. When we want to dive into the discomfort and push through, yet find ourselves unable, we can recognize the root of our discomfort is some type of limiting belief. We can then pull out our arsenal of deconstructing tools, go to work dismantling what has been holding us back, and break free into greatness.

THIRD: YOU ARE COMFORTABLE

This isn't as obvious as the last two clues, so it can be more dangerous, because it can sneak up on you.

Perhaps, you perceive no genuine area where you feel any limiting of your power. You think everything is going well. You hardly experience discomfort or fear. That sounds like a great life, but it must come with another truth. You are holding your deepest gift and impact back from others and perpetually avoiding offering your authentic self to the world.

You likely have subtle limiting beliefs keeping you stuck in the cult of comfort. At one point, you worked past your discomfort to get where you are, but the longer you settled, the more you became detached from your life mission, and the more you got lulled by your current success or comfort.

Maybe you have a good job. You don't like your job…you're definitely not fulfilled by your job. But you're too comfortable to move on to something better. Or maybe you're so comfortable in your freedoms and smoothly-running routine you resist the rewards of being in a committed relationship or having children.

Living out of your deep core to give your greatest gift will always be accompanied by discomfort. Living this way will inevitably expose limiting beliefs that must be worked through. This is just part of the growth process.

Some people choose comfort, because they've attempted to move past their current limiting beliefs without success, and the cognitive dissonance within (wanting to succeed, but being trapped by fear or limited power), eventually, was too painful. Success is redefined as something that can easily be achieved. And they get comfortable and settle…because believing they can do better is too painful.

This leads to a life of stagnation, eroding meaning, and loss of purpose. To be fully alive, you must pursue giving and allowing your internal greatness to be manifested. The more you ignore this, the more you will lack the aliveness, energy, and depth required to live a fulfilled life. And the harder life becomes. The more you detach from reality, the more you will hate yourself.

It is much easier, once you understand limiting beliefs, to live fully alive than only half alive.

Consider, are there areas of your life where you are stuck in a comfortable rut, simply sitting back and being comfortable? If so, you're probably being held back due to a limiting belief. It's ok to be comfortable for a short season, or if this comfort is merely support for other areas of growth, but an entire life in a comfortable rut is dangerous.

FOURTH: YOU TELL YOURSELF STORIES

Often we tell ourselves stories and excuses about our decisions in certain areas. The stories may try to explain why our "hands are tied" due to circumstances or other's actions or choices or why our response is justified, needed, or important. We will tell ourselves stories in these areas, even though we know we didn't act out of our true and deep power.

These stories aren't doing us any favors. They are feeding limiting beliefs, particularly beliefs that limit our ability to interact with the world in an empowered way.

Consider, do you tell yourself victim stories about your relationships, work, or spiritual life, blaming others in a way that takes the responsibility off your shoulders? Do you blame others for your lack of fulfillment in life? If so, you are likely covering up limiting beliefs.

FIFTH: YOU LOOK TO DISTANT OBJECTIVES TO HELP YOU WILL

FEEL BETTER

Someday, I'll have a great body.
> Someday, I'll do work I love.
> Someday, I'll be happy when I've found spiritual peace.
> Someday, I'll find my perfect partner.
> Someday, I'll be fulfilled when I have the finances to travel.
> Someday, I'll be in heaven and escape this miserable earth.
> Someday...someday...someday.

In this trap, we see a huge chasm between where we are and the "someday solution." We think something's wrong, so we stagnate in our dreaming, doing nothing, or we spend tons of time, energy, and money trying to fix it.

I've been caught in this trap often. I'm even fighting it now. I drop my boundaries between my work, health, family, and relationships. I convince myself, "Once I just build this...I'll have the money and time to do everything I need to do with my health and family." This is a fallacy. Achieving my goals in one area of life at the expense of other areas will always sabotage me.

Consider the business industry. Massive commercial markets are built around people expecting something external will cause them to feel better. From sugary drinks to cigarettes. Vacations to nice cars. Bigger houses, illicit porn, weight loss pills. All of these externals are marketed with the promise to make us feel better.

Be careful buying into that vision. It's a deep source of limiting beliefs, which will drive your actions, while simultaneously distracting you from the present enjoyment of your life and dreams.

STEP 2:

READYING

RECONTEXTUALIZE

THE

WORLD

FOR

YOUR

POWER

Everyone has one desire in common. To feel better.

veryone wants to feel better. It doesn't matter who we are, or what we do, everyone has this in common. Ultimately, everything we do is our best attempt to feel better. How feeling better looks is as varied as people are; it can be as different as feeling sexy or feeling holy.

It's important to realize this drive is foundational to who we are. Seeking to feel better is what got us to our current success. It has also made us vulnerable to limiting beliefs.

Because we always want to feel better, and we're not sure how, we constantly seek reasons we don't feel better. Our brain will give us two fairly consistent answers to that question. First, we believe we aren't able to feel better, because we have something wrong with us...and once we are fixed, we think we will feel better. And second, we think we aren't able to feel better, because we are missing something external in our life...and once we obtain it, we think we will feel better.

The next three chapters will address limiting mindsets that come when we expect ourselves to be better to be fulfilled.

The last chapter in this section will examine what happens when we focus on externals to bring us fulfillment.

5.

THE
END
OF
IDENTITY

LEAVING
THE
ESSENTIAL
BEHIND

To say 'I love you' one must know first how to say the 'I'.

A Y N   R A N D

Eventually, there is something we all have to embrace. The only person we get to be and to make decisions for, in the end, is ourselves. It is a universal conundrum. We have what we have. We are who we are.

My balding head, my struggle with work/life balance, my creative drive that wants to jump from project to project (too soon)...it's all mine. And this is key to understanding the source of my limiting beliefs.

Most of us, honestly, don't know how to live with ourselves. Sure...we have the basic things figured out. We know our favorite food. We may know a few hobbies we enjoy and our political or religious opinions. But we probably don't know our deepest gift to the world, so we have no vision for our life. We don't trust our own decisions, so we seek outside evidence to rationalize them. We don't understand our emotions, so we resist them. Ultimately, we don't love ourselves, so we stagnate.

This all perpetuates thoughts like:

> I'm not worthy of success.
> I don't deserve "the good life."
> I have nothing important to say to others.
> I'm not worthy to bring value to the world.
> I'm not worthy of an amazing partner.

Pretend your best friend is feeling similarly to you. Imagine you say to him or her what you say to yourself in your head. Are you shocked at the verbal abuse? I know my self-talk is often harsh. I'm not nearly as loving, graceful, or respectful toward myself as I am toward others.

This is a direct cause of limiting beliefs. Because we aren't often respectful and kind toward ourselves, it is easy to accept the stories our minds feed us.

You know the stories. The ones that tell us we don't have what it takes, it won't work out, and our very identity is the reason our life sucks. Our minds can only feed us these stories, because we do not love ourselves. So the first step in hacking these limiting beliefs is to build a context and foundation for understanding our self-worth.

If we don't love and respect ourselves, everything else disintegrates: our relationships, our work, our faith, and our dreams. We are the only filter between the world and ourselves. The more we doubt the filter, the more we doubt everything, sinking into indifferent apathy.

UNDERSTANDING THE COLLAPSE OF SELF-WORTH

Since you were young, you were trained to doubt your emotions and your choices. As a toddler, every instinctive action you made was monitored and controlled.

"Don't put that in your mouth!!!"...as a loved one grabbed something from your hand. This may have been necessary then, but now, to be someone who changes the world, you have to evolve past that. And the way you evolve is by learning to accept yourself.

Most of us have learned to seek the acceptance of others. We look to something else to decide our worth for us. This may be environment, circumstances, the church, God, mentors, Google, Facebook, our friends, what's popular (or not), and even books like this. So, we need not trust ourselves.

We're still the baby on the floor looking to someone else (or something else) to guide our lives. Are they applauding? Are they disappointed? We are still waiting for permission from others. We are still anticipating the removal of the object by anyone, not taking action because of what others may think or say or, perhaps, replaying the role of the adult from our childhood, "Don't do that! It might not be good! You might get hurt!" and constructing stories about all the horrible things that might happen if we take action.

This is just the beginning. Remember, once we accept something as true, our brain continues to look for evidence to "connect the dots" and confirm that truth. Our life's history is behind us and that history includes much that damages our self-esteem. We made mistakes, and many of us have a bucket list of regrets and reasons to distrust ourselves. Year by year, our mind has fed us a dizzying pile of stories, accepted without scrutiny, and attacking our self-worth.

These stories are often about:

- o Our biggest mistakes and failures
- o Our broken relationships
- o Our selfish manipulation of others
- o Our_____ (I'll let you fill in the blank)

When we were little, others told us who we were or who we should be and what was correct or not correct for our path. So now, we feel regret and shame for not being perfect (whatever that means), for making mistakes, or for hurting others. Then, we use that as evidence to prove we are unworthy and shouldn't be trusted. We hear and feel those failure stories in our subconscious mind over and over, whenever we want to step out and be great.

If you can relate to what I'm saying or see any of this in your own life, then you've put your finger on a foundational concept for overcoming limiting beliefs. You must learn to be ok with you. And not just ok, you must learn to deeply love and accept yourself.

Regardless of the people who pass through your life, the one person always present is you, so you might as well become best friends with yourself. You will have a constant stream of limiting beliefs until you do so.

You're an adult now. You're the one who decides what you put in your mouth, not someone else. You're the one who decides what you do with your life, not someone else. You're the one who decides if you have a great relationship with your partner, not someone else. You're the one who decides if you live with deeper purpose, not someone else.

Accepting yourself is the biggest step anyone can take toward removing limiting beliefs.

So, ask yourself, right now: Does your view of yourself work? Does it help you? Is it life giving?

Because if it isn't...I recommend trying a different idea.

Here's how...

6.

SELF-ESTEEM

ROCKET

FUEL

&

ROSES

The worst loneliness is to not be comfortable with yourself.

MARK TWAIN

This chapter won't be full of motivational, positive "hoo-rah." Motivation works for the short term, but eventually, can increase our limiting beliefs or become an addiction to something external. Instead, this chapter will cover some alternatives views, which can instill powerful thought processes, changing how you view yourself and the world.

TWO COMMON FEARS THAT KEEP US FROM ACCEPTING OURSELVES

FEAR *1*: IF I ACCEPT MYSELF, I WILL KEEP DOING NEGATIVE THINGS

Often people with this fear believe that accepting oneself means letting oneself off the hook and not being accountable to any standard. They believe that to "manage" their negative behavior or to hold themselves accountable, they must be harsh, angry, and shaming with themselves.

They may think things like, "If I accept myself...I'll eat a whole tub of ice cream in one sitting...I'll keep yelling at my kids...I'll stay stuck in my addicting habits (smoking, porn, anger, overeating)."

If you struggle with this fear, know that when you withhold love from yourself, you aren't keeping yourself from doing what you don't want to do. The reason for this is that all negative emotions (anger, guilt, shame, etc.) produce negative results. If you are filled with this negativity toward yourself, it will overflow in your life, and you will keep doing all the things for which you are berating yourself.

Love drives out fear, anger, guilt, and shame. Love will lead you to victory in all areas of struggle.

FEAR 2: IF I ACCEPT MYSELF, I WILL STOP DOING POSITIVE THINGS

Often, people with this fear believe accepting oneself means settling for the mediocre. Similar to those with the first fear, they believe that to achieve greatness, they must be harsh with themselves.

They may think things like, "If I accept myself...I'll stop working out...I'll stop trying to be the best person I can be... I'll stop growing my business."

If you struggle with this fear, know that true love for yourself will seek the best for you in the short- and long-term. Self-honor propels growth much more than self-hatred ever could.

These fears are two sides of the same coin, and the answer to each fear is the same. Self-love always gets us to where we really want to be.

I have had my fair share of struggle with these fears, and I have also seen great victory as I've worked through them. I used to feel like such a failure concerning money matters I would have a hard time discussing the facts of our budget with my wife, without taking things personally. I would shift from an objective and rational mode to an emotional survival mode. I couldn't take the heat, because I didn't accept myself, and feeling that pain was devastating. Once I developed a foundation of self-worth, I could discuss the realities or shortcomings of our finances, without feeling attacked or going into defensive, survival mode.

YOU ARE THE HEIGHT OF NATURE

You could have been a rock, a grasshopper, a tree, or something innate traveling through space. You could have been nothing. But you're a human. Out of over a trillion compositions on earth and an incomprehensible number of compositions in the universe...you exist. You're processing this, seeing this, thinking, feeling, and loving.

In this moment, you are breathing. Your heart is beating. That, alone, is a powerful miracle to ponder. Just think: here I am, somehow living, thinking and typing, and across land and time, there you are. Sharing in these words and ideas.

Ultimately, we didn't control how our own existence happened for us. How you are breathing where you are...and how I am breathing where I am. Yet, here we are, the very glory of nature.

If you allow yourself to recognize this wonder and beauty, there will suddenly be an inspiration in life unfolding within you.

You'll want to respond. You'll want to make the most of it. You'll no longer want to take it for granted.

This life is your single chance. You've already beat all of nature to get to this chance, so maybe, it's time to stop regretting and start living. Maybe, it's time to stop worrying about how others want you to live your life and start envisioning how you want to live your life. You are valuable, regardless of what you do or have. You are valuable, because you are here. Because you exist. And there is already greatness inside of you.

Allow me to take this a step further. For those who believe in God, this chapter on "loving yourself" may cause tension. On one side, you try to have faith that God views you through the lens of love and grace. But you are ridiculously afraid to view yourself in a positive light. You believe God loves you, yet hates your shortcomings (sin), so you think having "self-esteem" is a slap in God's face.

This causes many to align themselves with God through behavior, while strongly rejecting themselves as a person. This is living a life of contradiction, not faith.

Everyone knows "The Golden Rule", to love your neighbor as yourself. This ageless council presupposes you love yourself.

If you have any doubts of what "loving yourself" looks like, consider the famous "Love Chapter" (1 Corinthians 13), which lists what love is: Love is patient, kind, bears all things, believes all things, hopes all things, endures all things, rejoices in the truth, always protects, trusts, hopes, and perseveres...and love never fails.

Are you patient and kind with yourself? Do you believe and hope good things for yourself? Do you graciously endure your shortcomings? Do you rejoice in the truth of where you are, even if it isn't perfect? Do you protect yourself with necessary boundaries?

Do you trust yourself as a wealth of wisdom and knowledge? Do you always hold great hope for yourself and your future? Do you persevere in your growth process, always pressing toward your Edge?

Remember, love, not shame, guilt, or fear, begets the renewing of the mind and life.

THE GREAT PARADOX

I am nothing and I am everything, at the same time.

It's popular to approach "humility" as inadequacy and unworthiness and "confidence" as arrogance. Yet, you toning it down and playing small serves no one. Your greatness is bursting at the core of who you are.

Great joy and personal power is created when you can be humble (i.e., open to learning and different perspectives, admitting to not understanding everything, full of grace for other's realities) and confident (i.e., aware of your greatness, connected to your essence, and embracing your infinite abilities) at the same time.

ACCEPT BOTH YOUR LIGHT AND YOUR DARK

Part of the problem we have with self-confidence comes back to the principle of suppression. We suppress our inner darkness. We try to keep it hidden and secret, though we might violently swing toward it in certain moments to cope. This wreaks havoc with our identity, because it isn't authentic. It causes intense shame when we return to our dark over and over. It also screws with our heads, because we believe we have to be one or the other. But...

We need not choose between the two. We need to accept we are both. We fail and succeed. We are giving, and we are selfish.

We have moments of intense love and moments of intense anger or hate. Life isn't as simplistic as black and white; it's a struggle in the grey. We're in a growth process. We do things we don't want to do, and there is a constant choice and struggle between our dark and our light.

This is reality. And sometimes, we don't make the perfect choice. When that happens, the worst response is to keep it hidden and secret, instead of owning up to it and admitting we are in a process. When we keep it hidden, it schisms our view of ourselves and causes multiple limiting beliefs and self-esteem issues to arise.

When you embrace honesty and vulnerability about your darkness (whatever it is you aren't proud of), you allow a few things:

1. It is no longer "dark", because you are open and transparent about it, exposing it to the light. This immediately discredits your personal attacks on your own self-worth. Being honest is powerful.

2. Instead of being defensive, you become open to solutions. You begin to create what you want. Without an open acknowledgement of your darkness, it remains hidden, where it will not be addressed, modified, or battled with true courage and love.

3. You stop identifying yourself as the extremes: fully light or fully dark. You have the humility to accept you don't have it all figured out and the courage to admit your great worth.

YOU ARE IN A PROCESS

Our culture puts a lot of hype on "arriving" ... on finally, coming to a place where you have everything you need, are everything you want to be, and are perfectly content living the rest of your life in peace and happiness. But the fact is: You will never arrive. You are in a process that doesn't have an "end", a journey of continual change.

What the challenges look and feel like will change. The strategy and tactics will change. But the challenge of loving, giving, evolving, and creating?

It. Never. Stops.

This could be a disheartening realization. But, I hope you will let it be beautiful and freeing. When you embrace it, you realize you don't have to wait for the perfect life (like you've been thinking), but you have the perfect life—because you're alive and ever growing. You see how miraculous it is to be a human, tasting deeply of the highs and lows, the stops and starts, the sweet metamorphosis that is your life.

So, stop hoping for an arrival. Stop waiting to become perfect. Stop saying, "One day, I'll do this and that when I have more of this and that...." Learn to embrace the moment. Love, give, and grow however you can, wherever you are on your journey. Even if you don't feel ready. (Writing this book is a perfect example of me doing just that!)

This journey is new with each step. Instead of judging yourself by an imagined destination, judge yourself by how far you've come, and what you've learned about yourself. You are well on your way. Even if you fall down or take a wrong turn, only giving up is failure, and even that decision can be reversed in an instant, with a decision to get back up and start again.

So have grace for yourself. Have grace for not "arriving" and have grace to realize you are who you desire to be.

THE IMPACT OF FALSE STORIES

We've talked about how the feedback loop of your brain and emotions that form your perceptions of the world is an imperfect tool.

Your perception of yourself is no exception. Your entire life, your mind has been feeding you stories about your self-worth (or lack of it). By now, you likely have a predetermined picture of your self-worth. You automatically accept this picture as fact on a deep subconscious level. You don't even think about it anymore.

When I interviewed applicants for job positions, I came to realize my mind was making a snap judgment during the interview, within the first thirty seconds. I would unconsciously spend the rest of the interview trying to find evidence supporting that snap judgment. The interview may have been an hour, but in reality it would be an hour used to support my gut hunch, formed in the first thirty seconds.

What happened if my gut hunch was wrong? (Which scientifically happens over fifty percent of the time in interviews...) It didn't matter. My mind was connecting dots to prove my hunch, and if I didn't find evidence proving my first assumption right, I would go looking for it, even setting up guided questions to confirm my assumption.

This meant the interview process became as much about me as it was about who I was hiring. I had to implement a process to balance my "gut", because I desired to get the core truth of what was being said in the interview, despite my own internal assumptions.

Do you see where this is going?

Your mind has had a lifetime to pile evidence on top of the "truths" you have accepted about your lack of self-worth... "truths" rooted in extremes, rooted in your brain searching for a story, rooted in your emotions, and rooted in the emotions others have projected onto you.

Your lack of self-worth is a pack of lies, and you have spent your entire life collecting evidence to prove them true.

Thankfully, poor perceptions collapse, like a house of cards, when actively exposed to a better thought process. (We'll get to that soon.)

WE ALL DO OUR BEST

When I start sabotaging my self-worth, this statement is very helpful, "I did the best I could with what I had."

I believe this statement, now...but when I started saying it, I would think, "But did I really do the best I could with what I had? I knew better. I knew it was a bad choice, even as I made it!"

Yes. I knew better. But I still did the best I could.

Here is why. I am not just my mind.

It is common for our mind to argue with us as we make decisions. "You shouldn't do this...it won't be good." Yet, we still do it. Why? Because our subconscious and emotions are just as involved in our decision-making as our mind is.

A small example: We're standing in line for the most intense amusement park ride in the world; our mind is going crazy—feeding us possibility after possibility about how we might die. We still go on the ride and love it. Afterwards, we're thrilled. Proud. Excited. Confident. We don't question ourselves and say, "I should have known better," just because our mind was telling us not to go on the ride. We're proud we conquered and overcame the distraction of our mind's fear and negativity.

But what if the rollercoaster breaks down, or we hate the ride?

Then, suddenly, we made a mistake, and equate that to being a failure. We tell ourselves: "I knew I shouldn't have gone on that rollercoaster! I knew better!" Suddenly, we are filled with disappointment in ourselves, blaming and accusing.

See the setup? Our "failures" or mistakes have nothing to do with our identity. These mistakes simply happen when we make a decision to the best of our ability. When we feel at fault at our core, this is only our mind finding a story to explain pain.

You, all of you (including your subconscious and emotions), are always doing the best you can with what you have, even if you messed up and "knew" you were messing up as you were doing so. Yes. You will make mistakes. You are growing. Mistakes happen. So move the mistakes to the light, learn from them, and move on. Let the mistake teach you a lesson, and next time, you will do better. But don't let the mistakes define you. Don't suffer in shame. Don't hate yourself.

You did the best you could in that moment.

Because that is what you did.

If you could have done better in that moment, you would have.

AUTHENTICITY

What does "being authentic" mean to you? What used to come to my mind was the concept of transparency. Openly sharing the things I was ashamed of and being open about all my dark secrets and struggles. I thought that was all there was to authenticity.

Then, one of my mentors changed my entire perspective in less than thirty seconds. He said authenticity is you being the best you that you can possibly be. Your real self. Your powerful self. The self, deep inside of you.

That is your authentic self. That is your identity. That is where you are going. When you live out of that place, you are being authentic.

Everything else is just baggage hiding the real, authentic you. And when you define yourself by that baggage, you create tons of limiting beliefs.

When you are fully pressing into living out of your authentic self, you will change the world.

HAVING, DOING, BEING

How do you define yourself?

People default to an identity defined by possessions and behaviors. "Hi! I'm Bob! I'm a technical manager in one of San Francisco's most exciting tech start-ups. We recently got our third round of funding…" Or, "Hi! I'm Bob! I have a wife. I have children. I have an awesome Tesla car and a nice house. We regularly take vacations…"

I propose what you have and what you do have very little meaning, compared to who you are. What you have and do can quickly change. Who you are matures and develops, but the essence doesn't change.

Are you loving? Are you kind? Are you courageous? Are you imaginative? This matters. Focusing upon revealing your authentic self allows what you have and what you do to fall into place. Work harder on who you are than on what you do. Work harder on who are than on increasing your possessions.

THERE IS NOTHING TO FIX

This chapter began by talking about how everyone wants to feel better. The limiting belief may be that you will feel better once you fix yourself, but the reality is much simpler. You are amazing, and you already have a highly efficient vehicle for achieving the life you want.

You don't need another book, seminar, or coaching program. Though these can dramatically accelerate your process, you really have everything you need, right now, inside yourself.

Your work is simply realizing this. Your need to be different or to have something else to feel better is rooted in lies; you can feel better, right now, without changing a thing.

What's keeping you from being happy, right here, right now, in middle of your process? When you realize there is nothing to fix, you will know the answer is "Nothing."

7.

GET
OUT
&
STAY
IN

SELECTIVE
IGNORANCE
FOR
THE
HAPPY

If I am mentally in your business or in God's business, the effect is separation.

BYRON KATIE

W e have a powerful warning system hidden within. This system has the potential to warn us away from any thoughts, which will not benefit us. If we learn to recognize and honor this system, we will save ourselves from a huge amount of needless worry and distraction.

This warning system is nothing other than emotions. We can have "negative" emotions for many reasons, but one of the main purposes of these emotions is to warn us when we are meddling in something over which we do not have absolute control. If we feel anxious, trapped, or angry in connection to another person, our warning system is going off, telling us we have travelled past the boundaries of our own business, into the business of another.

Do we think about what God ought to do, what nature must do, or how the government should change? What about our spouse, our boss, or our friends? Do we struggle emotionally over what they should or shouldn't be doing? If so, how are these thoughts serving us?

This is a serious question to contemplate, because our minds will come up with many stories to justify our being in someone else's business. We need to be honest with ourselves. Are these thoughts helping those whose business we're in? Are these thoughts bringing us and others peace, happiness, and freedom?

When living in other's business, we will unknowingly tap into a huge source of negative emotions and limiting beliefs. This causes our minds to go to work, connecting crazy dots and building stories that will nearly always diminish love and life for everyone involved.

The kicker is, if you are constantly in someone else's business, you are not
paying attention to your own business.

So, next time you feel negative emotions and find yourself weaving a web of stories around people...

Check to see whose business you are in.

LOVING OTHERS UNCONDITIONALLY

How we view others is often a mirror of how we view ourselves.

Until we accept and love ourselves unconditionally, we may find it challenging to love and accept others unconditionally. Conversely, until we love and accept others unconditionally, we will be worried about what they think of us (since our thoughts are harsh and judgmental, we subconsciously expect others to be as well).

Grace, compassion, and an open mind and heart toward others follows extending these things to ourselves.

Consider...If you believe you are doing the best you know how...aren't they? If you have this battle of self-esteem...perhaps, they do as well? If you have these limiting beliefs...perhaps, they do to? If you had tough parents who negatively influenced your self-worth...is it possible they have similar struggles? If you are trying to feel better...aren't they as well?

People yearn to be accepted as they are, without a laundry list of expectations. Most people don't accept themselves, so when we accept them, without reflecting to them the judgments they've made about themselves, we demonstrate unconditional love.

By unconditionally loving and accepting others, we raise the entire playing field to a level of empowerment, instead of disempowerment, both for ourselves and others.

JUDGMENT IS ARROGANCE

A final word on judgments. It is easy to judge other's actions and decisions, but every time we do so, we also judge ourselves. We assume we could do better, given the same experiences, thought processes, history, relationships, and outlook as that other person in that single moment of time. That assumption is pure arrogance.

None of us know the sum of others' thoughts, subconscious drivers, and emotional drivers, much less how their relationships and experiences have shaped them. But every time we make a judgment, we lift ourselves up as someone who can easily and perfectly overcome inner blockage.

And of course, we can't. And when we don't, we judge ourselves as we have judged others. Judgment creates a viscous cycle of pride and arrogance, which plummets us into shame and self-hatred.

The escape is simple. We need to extend grace toward ourselves, and then it will naturally flow toward others. When we catch ourselves judging others, we need to realize we are creating limiting beliefs for ourselves.

We began Step 2 talking about how everyone wants to feel better. We've looked at how we try to feel better through fixing ourselves. Now, we will look at how we try to feel better by waiting for the externals in our lives to change...

8.

THE SECRET SHORTCUT

KNOW YOUR STARTING POINT

Let reality be reality.

LAO TZU

What is…is. What has happened…happened.

If you want to move forward, don't waste time questioning why reality happened. When you resist what happened, you will stay stuck. Accepting reality is the best place to start in recovery. Appreciate that it happened, and let the circumstances reveal and teach you what you need to know about yourself.

To read a map, the first thing you need to know is your current location. A map can't give directions to a destination, without first knowing the starting point.

We can assess our current reality and design a path to where we desire to be or we can play emotional mind games, imagining what should or shouldn't have happened.

I used to go weeks ignoring reality. I would wish for imaginary circumstances, becoming reactive, and passively waiting for things around me to line up. I would also go for weeks reliving the past, regretting what I had done or what others had done, and venting frustration about these little things. I told myself they were keeping me from living the happy life I wanted.

What a waste of my energy. I wasn't living in power. I was delusional and weak. I wasn't learning from what was happening. Instead, I was stuck in an imaginary world.

Embracing reality is powerful.

Don't spend your life regretting what has happened. Regrets steal the juice you could use to create a better future.

Accept reality. Here are some helpful tips...

APPRECIATE WHAT IS

Life is constantly swinging us crazy punches. It is easy to feel accosted and powerless. Yet, we are blessed with the choice either to embrace or resist all that life brings us. This decision holds great power.

We can go through hardships with a "martyr mentality." But will that change how things are going? How much control will we give to outside circumstances? How much of our happiness and identity will we allow to be dictated by something outside ourselves?

Those who survived the Holocaust had the choice to intentionally accept the reality of their situation. Their survival depended upon the attitude they formed around that reality.

Everything can be taken from a man but one thing: the last of the human freedoms—to choose one's attitude in any given set of circumstances, to choose one's own way.
VIKTOR FRANKL, HOLOCAUST SURVIVOR

If we do not move beyond accepting things as they are, we may disempower ourselves through passivity. How can we view reality in a way that neither victimizes us, nor leads us to passively observe our lives? How can we interact with reality in a way that is empowering and leverages us for personal growth?

We do so through appreciation. Appreciation is the added ingredient to accepting reality that can cause all things to be ultimately beneficial.

Yet, when we consider the darkest sufferings of humanity, it can feel like a stretch to believe reality can be appreciated. What about the premature death of a loved one, betrayal, rape, murder???

This is a challenge. There are horrific circumstances, which may not be appreciated in themselves. Yet, every circumstance has the potential to increase or stunt our growth, depending upon our choice. And it is this potential that can fill us with appreciation for all reality. Externally, we may be victims of great injustice, yet internally, we will never lose the gift of having control over our perception and response to life's happenings.

We can choose to seek—and scrounge if need be—for the benefits we've received from the challenges we've faced, allowing appreciation to encompass and fill our lives. When we do this, we are using reality for our benefit, regardless of the circumstances. This is powerful.

ACCEPTING YOUR INNER REALITY

When I talk about accepting and appreciating reality, I'm referring to more than the reality of external circumstances. I'm also talking about the reality of our inner struggles. It's powerful to accept these realities, to give ourselves permission to have them and appreciate what they are telling us.

With perceived weaknesses, we're often afraid to do this. We're afraid we will become overwhelmed or begin to stagnate. We don't know where the slippery slope of embracing our inner struggles will lead, so we try to ignore them.

Maybe we're sad. Yet, we don't want to admit or accept this, because we're afraid we will succumb to it. Maybe we are prone to be lazy...or self-centered. In these situations, we are acting like children, waiting for permission from someone else, not trusting our ability to manage ourselves. By admitting and working from our true place of reality and not fighting that reality within ourselves, we will find the emotion or weakness holds much less power than we feared. And once accepted, we have more clarity and strength to decide how to get to a better place. This is much more effective than pretending we are not weak in those areas, while our subconscious mind is continually demonstrating the truth to us.

Accept the reality of your weaknesses. They are your best feedback about where you can grow.

VULNERABILITY: THE SUPER POWER

Sharing our current reality with the world is quite freeing and de-stressing, once we get comfortable doing it.

I recently heard a speaker demonstrate this exceptionally well. In a talk given to a small group of people, he began with a timed minute in which he openly and vulnerably shared exactly what he was feeling and sensing in that moment: fears, selfish thoughts, doubts...whatever. This allowed him to get it out in the open, let it all go, and then freely give what he had come to give.

We'd be surprised how much we carry around when we are with others: the weight of not being vulnerable, not sharing our true insecurities or fears, and not sharing our true passion.

Vulnerability releases the weight, allowing us to be ourselves. Not only does this give us a basis for reality in our relationships, but it also increases our feelings of safety, because we are being seen for who we are.

If we are not vulnerable, we will have to play mind games in two directions. First, we have to deal with the insecurity that if people truly knew us, they would treat us differently. We feel like frauds whenever receiving love, appreciation, and power, and the good stuff others give us cannot land deeply. Second, if we're not vulnerable, the weight of not being entirely ourselves will be a heavy burden. We'll have the "job" of acting. We'll have less fun, feel disconnected and fake, and avoid expanding our boxes.

The risk of being vulnerable helps us, while bringing out the best in those around us. Everyone benefits. Everyone is empowered to evolve and grow.

Vulnerability is one of the most difficult habits to practice and develop. But it's also rewarding.

UP NEXT...

...We get down to the nitty-gritty. We've learned the foundation of the Edge Walkers path...now, it's time to unveil our arsenal of weapons for hacking all those limiting beliefs to pieces. Ready or not...

STEP 3:
EXPOSING

NINJA

HACKING

METHODS

USEFUL

FOR

THE

OBLITERATION

OF

LIMITING

BELIEFS

Spoon boy: Do not try and bend the spoon. That's impossible.

Instead... only try to realize the truth.

Neo: What truth?

Spoon boy: There is no spoon.

Neo: There is no spoon?

Spoon boy: Then you'll see, that it is not the spoon that bends, it is

only yourself.

THE MATRIX

We've worked through things conceptually, considering ways to process and think about the world. Now, let's get practical. We'll be doing real work, which will produce real results.

But only if you take action.

This section isn't meant to be simply read. When you have completed this book, I want you equipped to attack limiting beliefs and whatever may be holding you back. I am giving you effective tools to be used with focused intentionality.

If you're like me, you'll probably read the rest of this book, without doing a single "action step" or "exercise."

That's great. Do that. But then, come back to this step and use these tools to really work through the roadblocks you identify as you venture into the world with your gift. That's the whole reason you're here. Without taking these action steps, you won't be hacking your limiting beliefs. You'll just be learning about them.

While doing these exercises, don't be surprised if you get stuck in certain areas or have questions about how to move forward with a specific issue. If this happens, I recommend you look into joining The Unlimited Self group, where you can safely ask questions and get help when stuck (see Appendix).

Now let's get to it.

9.

HOW TO HARNESS THE POWER OF THOUGHTS

If you are distressed by anything external, the pain is not due to the thing itself, but to your estimate of it; and this you have the power to revoke at any moment.

MARCUS AURELIUS

The first tool to eliminate limiting beliefs is a process I call Freedom Hacking. This is a powerful process that puts you face to face with your limiting beliefs – and kills them.

Intentional devotion to implementation to this process can change your life in a matter of days. Many I know have experienced dramatic shifts and new inner freedom because of taking their long-held beliefs through this exercise. This process can often feel like the secret, magic key because of how simple, yet powerful, it can be in propelling you toward an unlimited life.

However, this process can be painful, because we are so attached to our limiting beliefs. Suspending belief in them long enough to examine them may feel impossible. So it will feel like work. You are developing a powerful life skill. At first, as you are practicing, it may not feel natural or very productive. It might not seem the process "works." But eventually, you will easily fly through these steps in a minute or two.

I find Freedom Hacking to be tremendously successful, but sometimes, the issue is deep and takes help or time to process fully. Further, not all beliefs are limiting. Sometimes, part of embracing reality is embracing the struggle we have with it.

Note: This process is adapted and modified from Byron Katie's non-profit system "The Work." I highly recommend her resources.

FREEDOM HACKING EXERCISE

Let's leverage the strength of your mind and emotions to your advantage. These step-by-step directions guide you through the process of separating "reality" from your inner stories, limiting beliefs, and emotions. When this happens, your brain and emotions simply "let go." What seemed like a massive struggle before will suddenly, almost effortlessly, melt away. This is the power of your brain and emotions working for you.

I am not naturally very introspective. If you're like me, you may have a harder time locating limiting beliefs by yourself and may benefit from walking through these exercises with a trusted friend or family member. Don't worry; you won't always need to do this...soon it will become second nature, and you'll be doing this in your own head, without even trying.

This process goes through six phases:

1. Uncover a belief

2. Write down the belief

3. Challenge the belief

4. Change in and out of the belief

5. Shift the belief

6. Evolve

So grab a pen, and we'll get started!

1. UNCOVER A LIMITING BELIEF

We want to find a single limiting belief to hack. Finding one may be difficult, because it requires examining what's going on inside. Perhaps, you already know limiting beliefs holding you back. If so, pick one, and skip ahead to the actual exercise.

In the second section, we discussed beliefs that crop up continuously. By reading the following list, you may find something specific you have been battling for a while.

You may have limiting beliefs:

o   In any areas where you feel as if your power is limited, and you can't be your authentic best (e.g., with your overbearing boss, parents, or partner)

o   In any areas where you feel deep fear or deep discomfort (e.g., cold calling, relational confrontation, or public speaking)

o   In any areas have you been comfortable for a long time (e.g., "okay" job or relationship with your partner)

o   In any areas where you tell yourself consistent stories about those around you or the world (e.g., "They—my partner,

family member, boss, God, government—
should/shouldn't...")

o   In any areas where you often seek externals to "escape"
(e.g., food, movies, pornography, alcohol, shopping, work,
"dumping" with friends)

Here are some other ways to identify limiting beliefs...

IN THE MOMENT

To find a limiting belief, wait until you're in a moment that causes
you internal stress or you are facing an obstacle. When you're
feeling those emotions, grab a pen and ask yourself, "Why?". Maybe
you've just begun your work for the day, and you're feeling stressed.
This may be because you have a limiting belief about making cold
calls. If so, ask yourself, "Why?" and start writing...

I'm feeling stressed.
Why? Because I'm not getting what I want out of my business.
Why? Because I don't want to make cold calls.
Why? Because I'm afraid.
Why? Because I feel like the people I call will reject me.
In this example, the last sentence would be a good example
of a limiting belief, "When I call people, I will be rejected."

FOLLOW THE SMOKE TRAIL

You can find limiting beliefs by becoming aware of your emotions.
Start where you feel emotions, like tension, anxiousness, fear, or
frustration - any emotion that feels constrictive in your body.

An easy way to find these is to allow a moment for you to take deep breaths. As you breathe deeply, you will shift your energy into body awareness and may feel constriction points in your body. Common areas include:

- o Stomach (which normally means an emotion of fear).

- o Chest/throat (which normally means an emotion of sadness).

- o Jaw/shoulders/neck (which normally means an emotion of anger).

Any time your body doesn't have peace, simply become aware and then ask yourself, "What am I feeling? Why am I feeling it?"

Your goal is deeper than just identifying that your root cause is "anger" or "jealousy." You want to discover the "statement" or the "why" behind the emotion.

Perhaps you've identified, "I'm angry at Jill for being late." You would then turn this statement into the underlying limiting belief (or beliefs). "Jill should not be so inconsiderate of my time."

Another example: "I'm sad I don't have the finances to go on vacation this year." The underlying limiting belief in that statement might be, "I'm terrible at managing my money."

USE A DUMP LIST

A dump list is simply brainstorming a list (on paper) of everything you believe or feel about something.

If you can't identify an area where you are limited, make a list of any area that isn't as amazing as you want it to be. As you examine your list, ask yourself which areas are the most significant and why they are making you upset. Your list will boil itself down to one or two main causes, which will be your limiting beliefs.

2. WRITE DOWN THE BELIEF

You now have an objective belief statement, regarding any area of your life that isn't bringing you peace. The statement should be past the stage of, "I feel frustrated that Jill was late."

It should be the reason you feel frustrated. "Jill should not be so inconsiderate of my time."

The statement you land on should be based on what you feel at your core, not on your thoughts while writing the statement. A childish and blunt statement is more effective at getting to the root of your emotions.

When I do this exercise, I often want to write down very blunt and "immature" things...and my brain goes into overdrive. "What?! I couldn't possibly be believing that...that's so silly..."

When your brain tells you stuff like this, it's a good sign. Keep the statement. It's what you really feel, and it's important you start with that reality.

Now, on a clean sheet of paper, write your statement. Then, we'll see how that belief statement stands up.

3. CHALLENGE THE BELIEF

This is a process of asking a simple question. (I'll give you the question in a moment.) There are no right or wrong answers. This is merely a Socratic process that helps bring a balance to what you are considering.

Question: *Is this 100% true?*

Sometimes, the very act of writing down a belief statement causes you to see the belief isn't true and you start letting go.

But sometimes, you may still deeply feel your belief is true. This is tricky, but I'll warn you, this step requires a good shot of humility and open-mindedness. Pride, arrogance, and pain will cause us to encamp on our beliefs, thinking we know all things and can see from all perspectives.

It helps to remember we only have one perspective. Seldom can we know that something is 100% true, because we don't know all the circumstances and intentions of others.

Using our example, "Jill should not be so inconsiderate of my time." When you challenge this belief, you may realize you cannot know for certain that Jill was intentionally being inconsiderate of your time.

If you still feel you absolutely know Jill should not be inconsiderate of your time by being late, continue to the next step.

4. CHANGE IN AND OUT OF THE BELIEF

You make sure the clothes you wear are comfortable and serve their purpose. This step is doing the same thing with your beliefs, with the pen and paper as your mirror.

Question: *Who am I with this belief?*

Write down how this belief makes you feel, what it causes you to do, how you treat others when you have this belief, etc. Be as thorough or brief as you desire.

With our statement, "Jill shouldn't be so inconsiderate of my time," you may write something like, "With this belief, I feel angry and taken advantage of. I don't want to associate with Jill. My stomach is in knots. When I'm with Jill, I avoid eye contact. Afterwards, I keep talking about how irresponsible she is."

Then, list how you would feel if you took this belief off, if it wasn't possible for you to think this thought.

Question: *Who am I without this belief?* Or, *Who would I be if this belief didn't exist?*

With our example statement, you may write something like, "Without this belief, I might feel peace as I wait for Jill to get here. Instead of making assumptions about her motives, I would be curious. I'd probably even be concerned for Jill, hoping everything is okay, remembering how stressful Jill's life is right now. I would probably have taken the chance to catch up on a good book or to cross something off my to-do list. When Jill got here, I would have enjoyed our time together and would have been grateful that I have a friend like Jill."

5. SHIFT THE BELIEF

Now, you will briefly try on alternative concepts to the belief and see if these feel as true (or truer) than your original belief. For example…"Jill shouldn't be so inconsiderate of my time."

Put yourself as the subject:
"I shouldn't be so inconsiderate of my time."

Switch yourself and the other:
"I should not be inconsiderate of Jill's (or others') time."

Change the belief to the opposite:
"Jill is considerate of my time."

If you think of other ways to change your belief, write them down, even if they seem silly. Some of the new statements won't fit, and that's fine. Just scrap those.

Once you have a few new statements, briefly take each claim through these questions:

Could this be as true or truer than my first belief?

When I try this belief on, does it feel better?

If you feel like one of your new sentences is true, but are struggling with it, it can really help to make a list of one to three things that make this new statement true. This helps, because often, your emotions will still not want to accept the new truth, so by scrounging for three things (no matter how trivial) that prove this statement to be true, you will suddenly expand your boxes. This part of Step 5 can be amazingly freeing. Just check out these examples:

"I should not be inconsiderate of my own time."

"...yes, this does feel true. Reasons this is true: 1. I was inconsiderate of my own time all day by stewing over how inconsiderate Jill was...I let it take over my whole day. 2. Just yesterday, I was inconsiderate of my own time in that I spent way too much time surfing the internet, putting me behind in all my to-do's."

"I should not be inconsiderate of Jill's (and others) time."

"...yes, this is also kind of true. Reasons this is true: 1. Because of my cold shoulder toward Jill, a part of her day probably sucked. 2. Sometimes, when Jill and I are hanging out, I dominate the conversation and talk her ear off – I see this is me being inconsiderate of her time. 3. I've definitely been late to a meeting or two at work and inconvenienced my coworkers."

"Jill is considerate of my time."

"I see where this could be true. Whenever Jill is at my house and sees I need to work/sleep, she is respectful of that and doesn't overstay her welcome."

Sometimes, a shifted belief will powerfully dissolve a limiting belief. It may also empower you with more empathy or an outside perspective.

6. EVOLVE: WHAT DO YOU WANT?

By now, you may find your original assumption has evolved or been collapsed. You realize it isn't as simple as you first thought, and there are other more empowering beliefs.

You're now ready for the final step: action.

Question: *What do I now want to create?*

In our example, you might write down: "I want a powerful connection with Jill today."

Question: *How can I create that?*

Walking out this action solidifies the shift from the limiting belief and you will feel powerful and expansive afterwards.

STUCK?

If you don't yet have freedom, attempt to determine if your brain and emotions have "shifted" to a different stance or belief. This happens often, when there is a deeper belief supporting the one we were first working through.

We deconstruct what we thought was the limiting belief, but then our mind switches to a new and more foundational limiting belief halfway through the process.

When this happens, return to Step 2 ("Write down the belief") and do the process with the newly uncovered belief.

It is possible to go through this process, without measurable freedom, due to the frustration of deep pain or abuse. However, taking true beliefs and legitimate pain through this examination can often soften them with a bigger perspective or temper them with more compassion and understanding for others. Again, even when everyone else would call us victims, we retain the personal power to choose how we respond. This process can help us choose a better response, one that feels better and helps us reminds us of our personal power.

Note: See the appendix for the Freedom Hacking Cheat Sheet.

10.

LEVERAGE THE HIDDEN POWER OF FEAR

I must not fear.

Fear is the mind-killer.

Fear is the little-death that brings total obliteration.

I will face my fear.

I will permit it to pass over me and through me.

And when it has gone past I will turn the inner eye to see its path.

Where the fear has gone there will be nothing.

Only I will remain.

FRANK HERBERT

If you think I will give you some platitudes about how fear is not real...I'm not. You know what I'm talking about. "It's all in your head..." "You're just imagining things..."

Fear is real. But just like thoughts or negative emotions, fear is data. The path to freedom is to be ok with feeling it, even if you're not sure why. By feeling it, you learn from it (if there is something to learn). By feeling it, you can leverage it. Instead of the fear making you weaker, fear will accelerate your ability and power by giving you unique clues to your growth.

Here is how.

UPGRADING YOUR FEAR (AND PROBLEMS)

The funny thing about fear is, even when confronted, it never goes away. Everyone faces it and everyone has it. But where they face it and have it...that's the kicker.

When I wanted to interview a guy I respected, I felt tremendous fear about asking him. It took me three days to get up the courage to send him the Facebook message. Then...it was done. Action won. What happened? Suddenly, I feared the actual interview. Same feeling of fear. Different circumstance. Now, I'm afraid of putting this book out to the world. (See how it goes?)

But let's examine something. While my fear in all three areas feels the same, my impact on the world in each area is very different. Asking someone for an interview has very minimal impact. Interviewing has more impact. And publishing this book has even greater impact. What have I done? *I've upgraded my fear.*

What is the difference between those who succeed and those who want to succeed? The 'wanna-be's' think fear will somehow go away, so they don't take action on small fears; they procrastinate. Some even procrastinate by "learning" outside strategies, skills, techniques, and approaches to eliminate the fear.

Those who succeed take action despite their fear, continually upgrading their fear. Once they feared talking to one person, and now they are afraid to talk to groups larger than 200. When 200 is comfortable for them and they upgrade to 500 (or 1,000), the discomfort feels the exact same as their initial fear of talking to one person. It feels the same as yours or mine. The fear doesn't leave.

The point shouldn't be to eliminate fear; the point should be to evolve, so you can take action, despite the fear. Fear can be managed by managing yourself (more on this later). But fear never leaves.

So upgrade your fear as rapidly as you can. Success will follow as the problems you solve also upgrade. Or keep your fear antiquated, always trying to eliminate the fear, and fearing the action steps that have very little impact.

When you've learned to upgrade your fear, the payoff to facing that fear is well worth it.

I should also point out, those who do not upgrade their fear, eventually, face an emotional package even bigger than fear: a perpetual feeling of hopelessness, a sense of being trapped, and daily inner pain and regret.

LEADING FEAR

Fear is often a byproduct of one or more limiting beliefs. Sometimes, it's best to address the fear head on. This is a technique I've used with various coaches, personally, and it has helped me manage my fear, so I could take action in many situations.

This technique is best done in a safe place with someone else leading, but it can also be self-administered. I will give the steps as though you are doing it by yourself. If you have someone else willing to lead you, they can simply use the script to guide you through the exercise. It is necessary to be in a place where you can close your eyes and concentrate on your own thoughts and feelings.

STEP 1: FEEL THE FEAR

This is critical, so whatever you need to do to feel the fear intensely, do it. Imagine yourself getting ready to do the thing you fear or if you need to, get ready to do the thing you fear until the feeling appears. Part of your body will physically feel different because of the fear. That part is trying to tell you something.

Once you have defined what part of your body the feeling is in (stomach, chest, throat, back of the head, deep gut...) and while you are still in tune with the feeling, rank your fear on a scale of 1—10.

STEP 2: MAKE THE FEAR TANGIBLE

This step helps us objectify our feeling into something tangible, so we can more easily engage with this part of ourselves.

Consider these questions:

o   What color is the fear?
o   What shape is it? (It can be anything...I've had spiky balls, fuzzy clumps, squares...)
o   How heavy is it? (on a scale of 1—10)
o   What temperature is it? (Ice cold to boiling hot)
o   Does the feeling make any sound?

Answer and let your subconscious serve you. There are no wrong answers. The "answer" is the first slight hint of something, so don't doubt yourself or question your instincts when you get a vague answer.

Now, in your imagination or mind's eye, the fear should have features that make it a "thing." (Sometimes, nothing comes to mind. If so, after one or two minutes, move to the next step.)

STEP 3: TALK WITH THE FEAR

Now that we have a "thing", let's dialogue with that part of our self to see what we can learn. This might feel weird or silly, but we will use our imaginations. Ask these questions with your eyes closed (eventually, you can do it silently). After asking, wait for a "sense" of a response. If you get no response after a few minutes of waiting, move on to the next question.

Ask the feeling, *"Are you willing to communicate with me?"*

All of our emotions can be a gift to us if we learn to listen to what they are trying to tell us.

Ask the feeling, *"What do you want?"*

Wait and observe what comes up. Don't expect elaborate answers to this question. Normally, they are one or two words, "feelings" or "pictures" you can easily translate into concepts or words.

Ask the feeling, *"Are you trying to help me in some way?"*

This is where I have gotten some large shifts. Because we suppress and dislike our fearful side, we forget our fear isn't something to be despised. Fear is data trying to tell us something for our own good. It's part of ourselves trying to help us.

When you ask this question, you may get a yes or you may get nothing.

Ask the feeling, *"How are you trying to help me?"*

During this process, your mind may try to play games and pull you off track. Keep the feeling at the center of your focus and see if anything comes up in response to the question.

Ask the feeling, *"Are you willing to help me without me feeling fear?"*

Wait and see if anything comes up. Ask the question a second time if you get nothing.

STEP 4: MAKE YOUR POWER TANGIBLE

With your eyes still closed, take your left hand, and using your imagination, pull the fear "portion" out of your body. Open your left hand, palm up, and let the fear sit in your hand.

Then, open your right hand and hold it out, palm up. Imagine your right hand filling with amazing and good things. Life, peace, love, strength, courage, nobility, gentleness, kindness, passion, bravery, expertise, boldness, energy, power, faith, pride, self-worth, authenticity, compassion, appreciation, and thankfulness.

Consider these questions:

- o   What color is this positive force?
- o   What shape is it?
- o   How heavy is it? (on a scale of 1—10)
- o   What temperature it is? (Ice cold to boiling hot)
- o   Does the positive force make any sound?

STEP 5: FUSE THE FORCES

As you continue to hold the two parts in your hands, ask them, *"Will both of you cooperate and form a super power that will help me achieve my goals, without being held back by fear?"*

Wait for a response. You might get no response or a negative response from your left hand. If negative, ask your left hand if it is trying to help you, or remember it is there because it is trying to help you.

Then ask them again. The resistance should be gone.

Slowly move your hands together and fuse the two parts together between your palms. Once the parts are fused into a new super power, place the energy back into your body, where it was originally located.

STEP 6: TEST THE RESULTS

Take a few deep breaths and then check the original feeling. Re-rank your fear on a scale of 1–10. Has the feeling of fear been reduced from your original number? You may find it has, and you have a greater sense of freedom and boldness. If it doesn't, run through the exercise again.

Once you are ready to exit the exercise, relax through a few deep breaths. Some people may feel disoriented for a few minutes.

TAKE IT WITH YOU

You can make a habit of calling up the right hand energy at any point in time to help you face moments of difficult fear or negative emotions. After doing this exercise a few times, you will increase your skill and be able to run the exercise in your head in just a few minutes as needed.

WHAT IF THIS DOESN'T WORK?

Don't expect this to remove all symptoms of fear. Expect it to lower the fear sufficiently to allow you to take action. I can normally get a 5 or 6-point drop (on a scale of 1-10).

If you see no results, you may try doing it with some of your smaller fears to increase your confidence and skill before attacking your deepest fears.

If you aren't seeing results doing this exercise alone, enlist the help of a friend and see if that aids your progress. Also, consider if you are judging the process as silly and naive. This would be a limiting belief.

Note: See the Appendix for the Leading Fear Cheat Sheet.

11.

GUZZLE THE MAGIC POTION

FORGIVENESS

What do you do with the mad that you feel

When you feel so mad you could bite?

When the whole wide world seems oh, so wrong...

And nothing you do seems very right?

M R. R O G E R S

Not forgiving is like drinking poison and expecting the other

person to die.

U N K N O W N

Forgiveness is fundamental to free your perspective and hack limiting beliefs. We can harbor unforgiveness in two ways: not forgiving ourselves and not forgiving others.

Some believe that to come to forgiveness, two people are required. This isn't true. Forgiveness is merely letting go of your negative feelings or thoughts of revenge, frustration, bitterness, and judgment towards the person who hurt you. Forgiving someone has nothing to do with the other person and everything to do with you.

Realizing the success of your forgiveness has nothing to do with an outside response is very freeing...it turns you from a victim into someone empowered.

Forgiveness doesn't mean you are condoning or accepting the action of another, nor that you are "giving up" on your perspective or truth. Rather, you are merely untethering yourself from the negative control that person or those events have upon your life.

Hopefully, this book is helping you gain perspective concerning both yourself and others, and you are already poised to forgive more easily. Here are a few additional concepts I've found helpful. We'll begin with self-forgiveness and then move on to forgiving others.

FORGIVING YOURSELF

We are usually unforgiving toward ourselves, because we are feeling either guilt or shame. We feel guilt when we desire to behave to our highest and best potential, but we don't. We are disappointed in ourselves. That disappointment can be a trigger for us to feel guilt.

Guilt is about specific actions, not about identity. I might feel bad for the way I respond to my wife. I wasn't being the best I could be. Guilt, in this scenario, is the feeling that helps me recognize I wasn't being authentic. Guilt clues me in, so I will pay attention, learn from the moment, take full responsibility, acknowledge it wasn't what I wanted, and grow into the best person I can be.

The first step toward forgiving yourself is simple: Has your behavior been less than what you desire for yourself? Do you desire to make amends? Do you desire to acknowledge you missed the mark? Should you move back to your place of power and communicate your willingness to take 100% responsibility for what you have done?

Realize you cannot control others. Others may need to express (in detail) how much you hurt them. Let them. They may also ask for you to take specific requested action. If it's possible and feels right...do it. But make sure that choice is yours.

They may not accept your apology. Don't get stuck in their business and don't let your freedom depend upon their positive response. You can only control your own thoughts and actions. Do whatever you can on your side to bring about forgiveness and then let go.

Many of us carry guilt about how we've treated our parents, siblings, or close friends. Writing them an honest letter of apology can be helpful. You can decide after you write it if you want to mail it.

Here is a simple letter format to get you started (include 1-3 things in each section)

1. Write what you're sorry for.
2. Write what the person probably feels due to your mistake.
3. Write what you would do if you could do it over again.
4. Write what you appreciate about the person.
5. After doing your best to make amends, if you still cannot forgive yourself, then you are dealing with something outside of guilt. You are dealing with shame. Shame jumps over behavior and lands in a person's core identity.

Shame says, "I'm not good." Or, "I am flawed." We all make mistakes. Shame empowers mistakes to define our essential self.

This differs completely from guilt, though sometimes, it occurs after ignoring guilt repeatedly and still committing certain actions.

While guilt may be a useful trigger, alerting us to failure, so we can behave as we desire, shame is never helpful. Shame is a massive saboteur of personal power and self-worth.

You are more than your mistakes, and even your shame shows that. You wouldn't feel shame if your true intention for yourself was not higher than your mistakes. That you have regret is a sign you're not happy settling with where you are.

BUT DON'T I NEED TO BE PUNISHED?

Feelings of shame often drive a person to desire punishment as penance—to escape or to be free of shame. If you try to deal with shame in this way, I would consider the question: Punished unto what end?

In principle, whatever you nurture will expand. If you nurture what is good and full of light, then life will expand. If you nurture what is evil and full of darkness, then death will expand. Which nurtures the good—you focusing on becoming your authentic self, or you focusing on punishing yourself?

When you punish yourself, where does life win? Where does good win? It doesn't. Punishment destroys life in you and in others. What do you learn by being punished? Do you not already know you made a mistake? Do we punish children who fail and fall at their first attempts of walking?

When you refuse to forgive yourself and attempt to punish yourself, the good you could accomplish by living your authentic self is limited and hindered. You can only move out of your mistakes and shame by moving into grace and forgiveness for yourself. This is the secret key to a transformed life.

One of my mentors says the following, "The greatest gift you can give to others is the gift of your own happiness." Your true, unique, and genuine self is a gift only you can give to the world. Shame keeps you from believing you have anything of worth to give. Shed the shame, so you can be the glorious human you are capable of being.

Note: Some people must deal with deeply implanted feelings of shame. I am not implying shame is always easy to resolve or even that it is only connected to mistakes we make. If you have serious issues of shame, you would benefit tremendously from outside help, and I strongly encourage you to seek the help you need.

EXERCISE FOR FORGIVING YOURSELF

Write yourself a letter of forgiveness. In the first part, take 100% responsibility for your actions. You were 100% in control of your ability-to-respond (response - ability). Be very specific about what you are forgiving. Then, write how you understand that you can't be perfect, and you were doing the best you knew how. Be extraordinarily gracious, kind, and understanding toward yourself.

FORGIVING OTHERS

I will say it again: When you forgive, you are not saying that what happened isn't wrong. Instead, you are taking 100% control of your reaction to what has happened and choosing to react powerfully in thoughts, action, and attitude.

It is well known that unforgiveness can deeply damage you, block you, and drive you into decisions not in your best interest.

Unforgiveness can even shorten your life. In your attempt to punish others who have hurt you, you punish yourself even more.

When holding onto unforgiveness, the act or person you are having trouble forgiving is literally controlling you and your life in that moment. Frustration at daily events (someone cutting you off in traffic) is you handing the control of your internal state and attitude over to others around you.

Just think of how much stress you are inviting into your life when you place control of your thoughts, emotions, and daily life, year after year, into the hands of others, who aren't even thinking about your best interests.

Don't fall into that trap.

By forgiving, you reinsert your control over your own life and make the best choice for your future.

EXERCISES FOR FORGIVING OTHERS

Probably, most of us immediately think of one or two people we have difficulty forgiving. Assuming you've done your best to make amends where possible, here are two exercises that may help.

MAKE A LIST

Make a list of everyone you can think of with whom you have an issue. These issues can be simple irritations or stem from deep bitterness.

Now, as you think of each person on this list, imagine an invisible chord around your heart running to that person's fist. Imagine them pulling the chord, squeezing your heart, and making the chord taunt.

Take a deep breath and imagine yourself cutting the chord and floating away freely. Actively forgive them and release your negative emotions about them. The old unforgiveness may crop up a few times in the following days...just go through this exercise in your mind each time it does.

If you have problems feeling freedom after this exercise, boil the issue down into a "should" statement ("My partner should listen to me") and do the Freedom Hacking exercise from Chapter Nine. Then try to cut the cord again.

WRITE A FORGIVENESS LETTER

Write a letter of forgiveness to someone on your list. Be honest and emotional in the letter. Tell the blunt truth. End the letter by listing a few things you appreciate about the person you're forgiving.

Then burn the letter. Make it a special ceremony and imagine cutting the cord and floating away freely.

CLARIFY THE OFFENSE

Sometimes, it is easy to become irritated or offended over small things that happen throughout our day. Your partner walks out of the room while you're still talking... someone cuts you off on the freeway...your child spills milk all over the sofa...your business partner doesn't respond to your calls all day.

When offended with others, we are withholding forgiveness from them.

A powerful exercise you can easily do in the moment is to clarify the offense (my wife swears by this exercise). Our ego is very good at blowing things way out of proportion and imagining everyone is out to hurt us. Often, once we look for other's best intentions, the offense melts away.

Whenever you get offended, say this sentence in your mind or out loud,

"I am withholding forgiveness from _____ because he/she _____."

The crucial key to this exercise lies in that last blank. If you just state the other person's action at the end, you will just reinforce the offense. Don't say, "I am withholding forgiveness from my wife, because she walked out of the room, while I was still talking with her."

Instead, imagine the other person's best possible intentions connected to their action. Search for where their innocent humanity could drive their actions, and insert that into the blank. "I am withholding forgiveness from my wife, Sarah, because she went to grab something in the other room and thought I knew she could still hear me talking."

A few more examples...

When someone cuts you off on the freeway, "I am withholding forgiveness from that driver, because they accidentally didn't see my car and merged."

When your child spills milk all over the sofa, "I am withholding forgiveness from my child, because she was just trying to use her curiosity and problem-solving skills to fix her sippy cup lid and accidentally spilled all her milk."

When your business partner won't return your calls, "I am withholding forgiveness from my business partner, because he is swamped taking care of important things, without a spare moment to call me back."

12.

REPROGRAM YOUR FUTURE SELF

Until you are happy with who you are, you will never be happy
with what you have.

ZIG ZIGLAR

The previous exercises were tools for dealing with specific issues. This chapter introduces multiple skills to quickly change your daily attitude, thoughts, outlook, and energy. If the previous chapters were like replacing a broken transmission, this chapter is changing your oil.

By now, you've learned how to build a better and more powerful space for yourself, your emotions, and your thoughts. You will have become more inoculated to the "stories" and triggers that bring about limiting beliefs or internal stress. These exercises are key for further evolving your thought-power.

BECOME AN APPRECIATION MAGNET

Recently, I had a conversation with Andy Drish. Andy has invested a great amount into his personal growth—working with life coaches, attending workshops, etc. So, I asked him what his #1 takeaway was. Without hesitating, he replied the most impactful action step he'd learned was keeping an appreciation journal. His mentor had stressed the importance of this to him, Andy had implemented it, and a year and a half later, he felt it was the smallest action with the greatest impact he could share with others. It literally changed his entire life.

How do you keep an appreciation journal? First thing each morning, develop the habit of listing a handful of things you appreciate. These could be things you appreciate from that moment, from the day before, or from a memory or future event. Anything.

Why does it work so well? Have you ever purchased a car (or considered purchasing a car), and suddenly, you see that car everywhere you go? The moment you focus your mind on something, suddenly you see the focus of your mind everywhere.

Now, imagine leveraging that power towards things you love and appreciate.

By focusing on appreciation first thing in the morning, you train your mind to see things you can appreciate all over the place. Suddenly, you see opportunities for great things all around you that you wouldn't have noticed before. You literally turn on your "magnet" ability to experience good stuff in your life.

Appreciation helps you maintain humility and gratitude for things outside of yourself...which helps your kindness and empathy. It helps you stay open to recognizing, believing in, and seizing opportunities...which helps your network and net-worth. It helps you stay focused on how beautiful life is (instead of how bad it is)...which helps keeps your energy and momentum up...which attracts awesome friends and better relationships...which creates more opportunity...which creates more to appreciate and be grateful for.

So, set the tone for your day. Keep an appreciation journal.

APPRECIATION VS. GRATITUDE

Writing an appreciation journal may feel too trendy for you...after all, it seems like we're hearing the benefits of writing "gratitude lists" all over the place these days.

It may be helpful to note the difference between appreciation and gratitude, so you can leverage the appreciation journal for your full benefit. I, and many others, have greatly benefited from this slight shift in understanding, and I hope it is helpful to you as well.

To understand the difference between these two words, it is helpful to imagine the posture of two people, one full of appreciation and the other full of gratitude.

The person full of appreciation is standing with their arms open and a free and unassuming smile. They are overwhelmed with thankfulness as they notice all their blessings. They are deeply content. This person realizes the ebb and flow of the gifts of life, so they have less of a sense of ownership over these gifts.

The person full of gratitude looks somewhat similar, because they are also thankful, but they are hugging tightly to themselves all they have been blessed with. They smile as their eyes focus on the things in their arms. They may feel entitled to their gifts, and there is a subtle anxiety in their heart, a small fear these things will be taken away.

Test this and see if you feel the difference for yourself. Think of something you are thankful for, and then say two sentences, one beginning with, "I so appreciate..." and the other, "I'm so grateful for..." If the differentiation between these words is not helpful to you, and you find the word "gratitude" helps you grow in thankfulness, then continue using it. But you might be surprised in the energy difference.

TALK TO YOURSELF

It is a proven scientific fact that thoughts and emotions influence the physical state of the body, and the physical state of the body can influence thoughts and emotions. This is a clue to a powerful tool that can influence your entire being: mirror talk.

Mirror talk creates a powerful energy loop by sparking powerful thoughts and emotions in your body through sound and vision. It supercharges your energy and positive emotion when you look at yourself in the mirror and engage in powerful statements about your identity and authentic self. It should go without saying, but if you mirror talk half-heartedly, you will not get these results.

Starting out, this exercise can feel cheesy. Just remember that thousands of people have used this one technique to leave the crowds of strugglers and rise in the ranks of the successful. You might consider joining us.

RECHARGE MEDITATION EXERCISE

By now, I hope you agree it is important to be aware of what is going on internally, both in your thoughts and in your emotions.

To do this, learn to be comfortable being with yourself and turning your mind "off" for moments of peace and silence. This is immensely rejuvenating and often brings to light some incredible information you haven't noticed, because you haven't had a moment to slow down.

I highly encourage you to take at least 15–30 minutes a day to be with yourself. Shut out all outside information and stimulation and just enjoy your own company.

Take a nap. Journal. Think. Draw. Sing. Be with yourself, just relaxing and creating in whatever way most rejuvenates you. Personally, I love journaling, while I'm outside in nature.

If you want to leverage this time for even more growth, here is a powerful meditation process that taps into the power of the subconscious to help you solve problems and gain specific insight into questions you may have.

When you're ready to do this, make sure you will have zero distractions for the next twenty minutes (turn off alerts on your phone and remove your laptop). This is time you have reserved to recharge you and access energy for your life.

PHASE 1: GATHERING AND GIVING

Lay down on your back or sit comfortably. Close your eyes and focus only on your breathing. This helps keep your mind from distractions.

As you inhale, gather your energy, bringing it deep into your body. Focus on the word "pleasure." This helps your brain focus on receiving. When you let out your breath, do so in a deep and controlled manner. Think about the word "energy." This gets your brain focused on giving. (These are words recommended by Jesse Elder, and they work great for me.)

You may feel very relaxed and a unique "aliveness" throughout your body. That's great—you are becoming more aware of your body, and your senses are responding to increased oxygen from your focused breathing.

Do this breathing for about two minutes, then move on to Phase 2.

PHASE 2: CONNECTING

Imagine where your life force is in your body. Many people will imagine it in their head or their heart. Imagine it as a white, warm, and loving light, slowly spreading and expanding throughout your entire body, filling it. Then imagine it spreading from your body and filling the room, your house, and the loved ones near you, and then your neighborhood. Imagine the love and life saturating and passing through every living thing. As the light spreads, imagine it spreading throughout your city...then your country...then around the entire planet. Feel yourself open and connected to the energy of all life, supported and supporting.

Take a few breaths, gathering pleasure and giving energy through this wave of connectedness. Move to Phase 3.

PHASE 3: APPRECIATION

Think about what you appreciate. Consider the last twenty-four hours and then allow yourself to go back to any point in your life experience: people, accomplishments, events, wins, special moments—it doesn't matter how huge or small— just appreciate them. This positive focus, acknowledging what good things have happened to you, helps place you in a state of positive power.

When remembering what you appreciate, make the memories vivid (try to remember all five senses and any emotions you felt). Let the feeling of appreciation ripple through your body.

After you do this for a minute or two, move on to Phase 4.

PHASE 4: TRAILBLAZING

Now imagine your unique future in three years, giving your brain, emotions, and subconscious the opportunity to help you make it happen. We overestimate what we can do in one year and underestimate what we can do in three years.

See moments of joy, beauty, achievement, success, and strong relationships. Imagine smiles and laughter. Moments of intimacy, deep friendship, and breakthrough. Imagine big numbers in your bank account, exciting adventures, and being fully alive, doing your passion. Imagine being the friend and family member you want to be.

This is a free-flowing imagination exercise. Try to imagine using all five senses. Mentally explore your ideal health and body, your character and outlook on life, your family, friends, activities, achievements, skills, and how you are contributing to others. Blaze an amazing trail in your mind as you imagine your reality three years from now. After a minute or two, move to Phase 5.

PHASE 5: FUTURE PACING

Now, imagine your next twenty-four hours. What needs to happen to help you achieve your three-year vision? Step through your day, imagining each step, resulting in the best possible outcome. Focus on your day's top or most-feared priorities and imagine them happening without a glitch.

Once you've imagined your whole day, return to the gathering and giving breath from Phase 1 for a moment.

PHASE 6: RECEIVING

This can be the most powerful part of your twenty minutes.

This phase is simply seeking, asking for, and waiting for wisdom and insight. During this time, I seek God. Those with different worldviews may seek the wisdom of the subconscious or life force.

After establishing your breath, simply ask: "What do You have for me?" And wait.

In asking this question, you are embracing humility and laying aside your ego to open yourself to new concepts and thought processes. The gift may arrive as an answer to a problem you are facing, an incredible idea, or the face of someone you know you should contact. For me, it has also come as a Bible verse reference or page number to look up.

Whatever it is for you, this moment can be powerful. These are moments I feel God giving me direction or divine wisdom. Don't be afraid to ask hard questions and wait for the "still small voice."

I frequently journal these "conversations" with God, or I write down the idea or solution given to me during this time.

Once the dialogue has subsided, imagine God's creative energy filling you, loving you, hugging you, and supporting you.

Exit the meditation through a few more gathering and giving breaths.

Note: See Appendix for Recharge Meditation Cheat Sheet.

CLOSE THE GAP

Having a constant list of "shoulds" in your head will quickly drain your energy. This is something I constantly battle, and I call it "the gap."

The gap describes the space between where you are and where your mind thinks you should be. This is the gap between a thought commitment to something that sounds nice, but is a challenge to achieve, and what you actually do.

Perhaps, you're in the middle of a work day and a "should" comes to your mind. Maybe you've been wanting to call and catch up with a friend, or you feel the need to wash your car, work out, do taxes, write new goals, etc. These are things you want to do, but cannot do immediately, so they are just creating many "gaps" in your mind throughout the day. At the end of a fairly successful day, you may still feel like a failure and overwhelmed because of all these "shoulds", which you've been unable to accomplish. Your mind can quickly feed you a virtually impossible to-do list.

Unless you become intentional about letting go of all those "shoulds", you continually expect those things of yourself, without even thinking. This gap will kill your self-esteem, stifle your creativity, and cause anxiety.

Here is the solution.

Close all gaps by questioning your "should." Do not mentally commit to anything, unless you write it down. If you hear a "should" creep into your mind, stop and double-check yourself. If it's truly something you want to do, write it down somewhere, so you can track and cross it off. But usually, you'll find the "should" isn't as high of a priority as something else you are working on. If so, take it off your mental commitment list and refuse to accept the "should" your mind is feeding you.

Another solution to closing the gap is a free app called WinStreak. Use this app to post your wins for the day. It takes two minutes, and after several days of tracking wins, you feel good about what you've accomplished. Therefore, you are much less vulnerable to all the false "shoulds" your mind throws at you.

JUST A SLICE, PLEASE

Sometimes, giving our gift starts with a simple question, "What's the smallest action step I can take, right now, to move me forward?"

Slice your big action steps into small wins and celebrate those. This builds your steam and your self-confidence.

I heard of a guy who had so many limiting beliefs he could not do anything. So he hired a powerful coach. The coach asked him to commit, beyond a shadow of a doubt, to a specific, simple action-step each day. The client was eager to do everything he could to change...and eagerly awaited the assignment.

"Make your bed."

What?

"Make your bed. Every morning. Call me in a week."

The coach understood that, sometimes, people just need a little traction. Once we start something, we rapidly pick up steam. But simply beginning isn't always simple. We create a massive event in our head and fail to start, because we've made it into such a challenge.

Taking the first small step perpetuates us into getting something done.

So start with something small to get traction. Once you have traction, you can grow your action steps. But even winning with small actions consistently can accumulate into a big win. If you swing for a home run every single pitch, you're likely to fail. But if you learn how to hit a single consistently... the bases get loaded, and you hit a home run with every single the rest of your life.

DIRECT THE ENERGY

This is pretty straight-forward, so I'll keep this one brief.

Sometimes, you're fighting strong negative emotions, like doubt, fear, discouragement, or anger.

Outside of the tools I've already mentioned, don't be afraid to release that negativity in physical activity. Run. Lift. Punch. Play a musical instrument.

Unloading on those around you isn't very nice, and holding it in is unkind to yourself. So take an hour or two and work it out through physical action.

STEP 4: EMERGING

ON

THE

FINDING

&

GIVING

OF

YOUR

GREATEST

GIFT

Do you want to be happy? Try helping someone else.

UNKNOWN

Here is what I don't want. I don't want this book to cause you to be so focused on your internal state you never live life on your Edge.

It's human nature to "get ready to get ready", so some people will take tools like this book and become addicted to seeking little cracks in their life, endlessly "working" on themselves...just so they will be ready to live.

Your mind can find thousands of limiting beliefs. You can find a negative emotion behind every moment and fear around every corner. You can dig into your childhood and unearth wound after wound.

Being addicted to that endless pursuit misses the entire point. It relegates your power to something outside your control and keeps you from giving your best gift to your loved ones and the world.

You are ready to take action, now. You are ready to give, now. You always have been.

These tools are unto something. They aren't an end unto themselves. If you get stuck working on yourself, without giving your gift to the world, you won't find happiness, you won't find joy, and you'll never experience an unlimited life.

As Braveheart says...everyone one of us dies. But not every one of us truly lives (or loves). Not everyone one of us feels the happiness found in serving others or risks giving our gift to the world.

There isn't much difference between someone who gets stuck running in the "personal growth treadmill", and someone who is indifferent. Both are navel gazing. Both are unfulfilled. Both refuse to take action, and both leave the world void of what they could have given. Don't let that be you.

This section is about taking action and inspiring you to be who you were meant to be.

These are the final keys to living the unlimited life.

13.

DISCOVERY

SET

SAIL

Know the truth of who you are. That is the truth that will set you

free.

CHRISTOPHER J. STUBBS

Discovering the unique gift you will give to the world isn't always easy. You've heard it from me, and you've heard it from others:

Follow your passion!

Do what you were made for!

Give your gift to the world!

But what if you don't know your passion, purpose, or gift? What if you don't know what you love? Then this chapter is for you. I don't want you limited and stagnating any longer.

When I was thirteen years old, I decided I wanted to be a business owner. It only made sense. Business owners seemed to make the most money, be in control, and have the most freedom. With the support of my parents, I started a lawn care company. Several years later, I had created a great job...that I hated. I was dissatisfied, but blamed this on myself. It took me years to determine that my lack of passion in my business had nothing to do with a failure on my part and was simply rooted in me working outside of my strengths.

So I learned something about myself. And moved on. My dream of being a business owner didn't die with my failure to build a massive lawn care company. It just evolved. I simply wasn't cut out for the repetitive service industry.

My point is this.

We're only sailing.

Imagine you're in a boat in the middle of a large lake. Far off, in every direction, you can see the shore. If you're living without purpose, you don't control the set of the sail or your rudder. You just go where circumstances take you. Sometimes, you sit doing nothing; sometimes, you're blown to the south, sometimes, to the north.

When you decide to find your passion and purpose, you set your sail, grab your rudder, and aim for what seems to be the best shore in that moment.

As that shore gets closer, you might make out some details. Maybe you don't like how it looks, and do a 180, choosing another shore. Maybe you love parts, but a little further south looks better. Maybe you love it, and you keep going.

Based on what you learn, you adjust your rudder and continue to sail.

Does your core passion or purpose "change"? No. You're just evolving with better knowledge and data about where you are sailing. The more you evolve, the more you can finely tune into your unique and special gift. The more you give, the more you learn. The more you pursue (and fail) the more you realize what you were made for and what you weren't made for.

Everything up to this point in your life has helped you map what you think will be a fulfilling shore. From here, the more you take action, the more you can dismantle the limiting beliefs around your gift and passion.

That's why failing fast is awesome. You quickly discover who you are and aren't. Obviously, you don't intentionally sail towards a shore you don't want (failing on purpose). But it's perfectly ok if you arrive at a destination and realize it isn't for you.

Giving your gift and living out of your passionate purpose is an ongoing, organic process that evolves with you. You may have something you are passionate about, right now, and that might change in three years. That's ok.

The destination is merely part of the process. The main point is simply that you have your hand on the sail and rudder, and you are actively deciding to live your life and give your gift to the best of your abilities.

THE FOUNDATION: YOUR IDENTITY

A perspective that has helped me immensely in my search for purpose and passion is an answer to the question: Who am I? I would invite you to consider this simple answer can change everything.

At the core of who you are, more than anything else in the universe, is a creator.

Here is why.

First: *Like begets like.* You were made "in the image" of God - creative power is core to who you are. An oak tree doesn't give the world cherry trees. A deer doesn't give the world rabbits. If you believe, on any level, in a Creator, or a higher power - it's safe to assume you have that creative power in you. You have the will to expand life and create new things around you. And I'm not just talking about art, or music, or painting (though that is included). I'm talking about the entirety of your choices and experience. It's all a creative process. Your design is to expand, create, and occupy.

Second: *Nature*. If you don't believe in a higher power...I would invite you to consider that, of everything we know in nature, we are best evolved and equipped to create. We have the minds, self-awareness, and the imaginative power possible to create, unlike anything else we have yet discovered. You evolved to be a creator. It makes sense that you would be most fulfilled being one.

So what does this mean? The problem is simple. Most of us don't trust ourselves as creators. We grew up doubting our own power, minimizing it, and believing we were victims to outside circumstances or people. We refuse to take 100% responsibility, and in doing so, subject our creative power to others.

When we live outside of alignment with our created or evolutionary design, we will feel opposite of expansive. We feel constrictive and stressed, like something is wrong with us.

When we live according to our design, we feel expansive, free, and happy.

It isn't as much a question of what we want to create. The question is much more simply: are we choosing to create moment by moment? Each moment contains millions of choices. Do we approach life with this creative energy? Or do we usually feel we are stuck between only two choices?

The sooner you realize you are a creator with infinite ability and possibility in front of you, the sooner your passion and purpose will become even more apparent.

FINDING YOUR GIFT:
PRINCIPLES AND CONCEPTS

With that perspective in mind, here are a few things that will help you discover your shore and tap into your inner dreams and passions.

STOP WAITING AND START ASKING

Find a time when you won't be disturbed for fifteen minutes.

Close your eyes. Relax and breathe deeply.

With your eyes closed, ask your "feelings" or "gut" these questions out loud. Wait for a response for each.

1. *What do you want for me?*
2. *What kind of gift do you want me to give to the world?*
3. *What's the first thing I can do to work towards this?*

See what type of imagery, thoughts, ideas, or words come to mind. It might help to write them down. If writing them down disconnects you from your feelings, record a video on your phone of you doing this and speak the answers out loud.

Ask follow-up questions, if applicable, to get details.

ASK YOUR MIND AND SUBCONSCIOUS POWER

This is something one of my mentors recommends.

Every morning or evening, write the following into your journal, "I want to know what I want."

Throughout the day, don't forget to jump back to that statement, offering it to your mind and subconscious to give you answers.

Answers will arrive randomly, while in the shower, while driving, while working. Jot them down in a journal.

After a few days of considering this statement, take another fifteen minutes to sit down and explore the answers in your journal.

This leads to the next concept...

GO INTO THE WOODS

Imagine your life path leads through a deep, dark wood.

Up to this point, you have probably walked the same paths as everyone around you. It might be the "college" path, the "good job" path, the "get married and have kids" path, or maybe it's the internet marketing or blogging path.

Whatever it is, maybe you've seen these strategies working for others. So you've copied what they've done, and you've imagined their results for yourself.

But the copying thing only works for a small percentage of people: those who take the principles and carve out their own path with the wisdom of the principles in mind.

Why is that? The reason the successful could succeed is because they were blazing a trail.

Here is my point. Your gift and how you give it will be unique. It won't look like anyone else. It won't be an exact system, formula, or concept you can just copy-cat, or that others can copy-cat off of you. A massive element of attracting success is you being you. We're talking about *your* gift. *Your* path.

That means, obviously, it will be scary. It's going to be unique and uncharted. Because it's your Edge, it's a path no one in the world has ever taken.

This is very exciting, but it also means that, when you ask yourself what your passion is, and anytime your feelings offer an exciting "live life on the edge" idea...you will experience the emotional rollercoaster. A high of excitement when you imagine how amazing something could be...and then...a low as limiting beliefs, doubts, and fears flood in.

That's where this book comes in. The more you can recognize and work through the lies that limit you, the more you can live out your greatness and blaze your own trail. Success comes to the trail blazers!

FIND WHERE YOU'RE A NATURAL

Giving your gift to the world can be intimidating, because you're assuming you have something of value to give and that people want or need what you have to give.

To cut down the intimidation factor, find where you already help people naturally, and where you feel proud and fulfilled afterwards. This can offer insight into how your gift to the world might operate.

I tend to be detailed and extensive when teaching or giving my advice, direction, or input. I can go on for hours, and time flies, especially in one-on-one conversations. I love learning and sharing what I learn and seeing people walk away with clear understanding and excitement.

However, I'm not someone who likes doing specific actions for people. I can and I have, but the time drags. Other people I know love cooking great meals for others, or helping with the dishes, or helping repair or build something. Even others like "managing" big projects unto a greater purpose or solving a big problem through smart action.

Where do you help people? What do you enjoy about the process? This might be a big clue to how you will give your gift to the world.

HOW COULD YOU HELP ONE PERSON RIGHT NOW?

Can you think of anything you are passionate or skilled in that could help others? If so, try giving one hour this week to help someone with that one thing (as long as it will make you feel more alive and you will enjoy doing it).

Who can you help first? Should you send a Facebook message, text, or call make this happen? Do it. You might find it is the best hour of your week.

DEVELOP SKILLS

Over the past ten years, I have developed several skill sets to pay the bills while I experimented to determine and evolve my personal gift to the world. I purposefully chose each skill, because I felt they would help me develop the larger gift I had a vague idea I wanted to give. This meant I taught myself in these areas: running my own businesses, sales, leadership, management, web design, marketing, psychology, internet marketing, negotiation, hiring, copy writing, communication, parenting, and others.

The trick is finding skills you love developing and you know will help you give your gift with more impact.

You may find your skill-set isn't taking you where you want to be. This realization is part of the reason I finally left my lawn care company. If this is true for you, trim your sail and find a new skill set, which will get you closer to the shore you desire.

Remember, everything is connected. No matter your skill, there is something in that skill-set that can be correlated to your passion and gift. Though you may not use a certain skill, you will still benefit from the discipline you exercised, networking connections, or some other aspect that grew you in important ways.

Further, building a new skill set need not be overwhelming. Forget going to school. Find internet videos, experts, and mentors from around the globe. You can easily accelerate your learning and be in a very successful, skilled position in six months to a year.

14.

FIGHT THE TIDE

Choose friends who are themselves living at their edge, facing their
fears and living just beyond them…

D A V I D   D E I D A

The next best thing to being wise oneself is to live in a circle of
those who are.

C. S.   L E W I S

When you live on your Edge, the world and even your closest friends will probably look at you like you're crazy. And then, when you "make it", they may admire you…but then many become scavengers. Living on your Edge can be lonely.

That is why you need worthy friends through your entire journey. Friends who know the depth of your weaknesses and strengths, can see through the lies you tell yourself, and who know just how to help you when you're stuck.

Regardless of where you are in your quest for greatness, you probably don't know of many people setting their dreams as high as yours. And you're probably wondering if you are crazy.

I'm here to say—yes. You are crazy. And it's vital you find other crazy people like you. There are many more of them out here than you think. You need to find them. You may build relationships with them or simply read the content they put out on a blog or Facebook.

When you stumble across these kinds of people, you immediately feel alive. They can exponentially accelerate your progress, give you insight into how to fight your battles, and inspire you to take the next necessary step.

To walk your path with success, you will greatly benefit from coaches and mentors.

You can also take advantage of books, videos, blog posts, and podcasts. Steep yourself in these resources. And take the principles and apply them towards your own gift. Don't get stuck in "information overload" addiction, or "waiting to get ready" syndrome, where your limiting beliefs about perfection and doing it right cause you to consume information for years, instead of taking real action. Getting stuck in this trap will destroy your self-esteem, because it constantly builds that "should" list in your head (I've been there, too).

Doing is where everything that matters happens. It's crazy; even in paid groups, 80% of people don't implement what they purchase. Find quickly a support system of powerful people who will help make sure you're doing what you are learning.

A great starting place is my private Facebook group, The Unlimited Self: **www.facebook.com/groups/theunlimitedself/**

15.

SURRENDER

&

OPEN

HANDS

To know God, without being god-like

Is like trying to swim

Without entering water.

 O R E S T   B E D R I J

S ometimes, we hit a place where our will isn't enough to get us unstuck. At this point, we need a higher energy to pull us up. This may be a good friend willing to sit with us, hug us, listen to us...just be with us. We can be lifted through that energy, which is love, compassion, and life.

Sometimes, we can't see the forest for the trees, and the only energy we have within is the energy to surrender. In that moment, we can pray. We can walk into nature and reconnect with the God, who deeply loves us. In this great Presence, we can let go of everything, surrendering ourselves to God's hands.

Often that choice, for me and countless others, has been the spark that has lifted our consciousness, given us life, joy, and an outside perspective. And given us the faith and the hope to keep fighting.

I encourage you to set aside an afternoon and try it for yourself.

Go to a place of beauty and peace and surrender to God. Open yourself to a flood of love and allow yourself to let go of any limiting preconceived notions. With the innocence of a child, ask God to be your friend. And just see what happens.

I know my life wouldn't be the same without this relationship.

There is a depth of freedom, insight, and power in my relationship with God that isn't to be had elsewhere. I don't pretend to know why or how...only that it's true.

EMBRACE THE PARADOXES

It's easy to think in terms of "good and evil" or "black and white." But life is full of paradoxes. Life is mostly grey.

For instance, you are a speck on a speck next to a speck hurdling through space. Compared to the immense size of the universe and scope of time, you mean little.

On the other hand, you are powerful, and in your inner being have an immense gift to give to the world. You are a unique individual at this special moment in time. Your impact on your loved ones and all those you touch in your lifetime is immeasurable.

Said another way: Wisdom tells me I am nothing; love tells me I am everything. By embracing both, we can learn something.

Paradoxes surround us. When you give your gift, you will need to be comfortable with juggling them.

I want to leave you with a final paradox: the power of letting go.

Chasing your dream is a tightrope balance of taking the right action and emotionally letting go of the future. In more detail, it's about realizing you are whole and complete just the way you are, but part of your identity is to expand and create. However, expanding and creating doesn't mean you get **attached** to the outcome of your creation. Your creation doesn't define your identity or worth.

Leave your hands open for what you may receive...and open for what you may lose or give. Grow. Evolve. Give. But leave your hands open. This attitude allows for flow...and where there is flow, there is life. Don't walk up to the river of life and try to grasp tightly what you want. Walk up to the river, cup your hands, and wait for the water to pour in. When it pours in, the water will fill your hands and then overflow. The minute you seek to grab what enters, you will stop the flow. As you leave your hands open, the life-giving flow and overflow will be continuous.

16.

100%

RESPONSIBILITY

FOR

THOSE

IN

COMMITTED

RELATIONSHIPS

Love begins at home, and it is not how much we do, but how much love we put in the action that we do.

M O T H E R   T E R E S A

1+1 equals 11.

C H R I S T O P H E R   J .   S T U B B S

Your first place to give your gift, your testing ground, your first external arena...is in your home. If you are in a committed relationship or have kids, this is your testing ground. This is the first place for you to give your all, to release who you are, to love with abandon, and to serve. This will be your biggest training ground and could be your greatest victory when all is said and done. This is where you will suffer the greatest defeats and reap the greatest rewards.

Your family knows the real you, beyond your game face.

While you can only give what you have, the reason you become more is so you can give more. The moment you stop focusing on giving is the moment you stop becoming.

You cannot become love, without giving love.
You cannot become great, without sharing greatness.
When you expand, you include others.
When you live life, instead of indifferently coasting through it,
you touch others.

Your family is first in all of this. If you cannot level up at home, it is only a matter of time before you will fail to level up elsewhere. Ignoring your gift at home, ignoring the call to give your best, ignoring vulnerability, ignoring honesty and not facing the hard things will put limiting caps on your future.

Home teaches and prepares you for the world. Your lover can be your greatest gift and your greatest source of struggle. And like most things in life, your perception will decide what you believe about your partner.

Many who start deep-diving into their personal development feel the foundations of what they thought they wanted shaking. They may doubt their relationships, suddenly seeing they aren't caring for themselves, being honest, or feeling safe enough to be their authentic self.

Often, the personal growth phase doesn't happen at the same speed for couples. Sometimes, one partner grows leaps and bounds ahead of the other. If you are the one in a season of growth, be patient and ready. Readily pour out love, grace, and forgiveness.

Any relationship of commitment is all in. And the only "all in" you can control is yours. So, if you're struggling and doubting your own happiness in your relationships, you are being tested. Your relationship is doing what it does...forcing you to grow and exposing your darkness.

Recommit. Level up. Communicate when it hurts. Build boundaries if needed. Love and give. Be your authentic self with those you love most.

Don't let your life pass, without knowing you gave your all on the arena floor.

FINAL THOUGHTS

At the end, there is only one simple decision. You can either give your best to the world... or give up.

The world needs you fully alive. We need your unique outlook, insights, and strengths.

When you float through life, believing you aren't worthy, your gift isn't worthy, or your voice doesn't deserve to be heard...you are doing one of the most selfish and cowardly things you can do.

I want to inspire you. Because, before you know it, your children and grandchildren will be crowded around your bed as you realize you've come to your last breath. In that moment, you don't want to have regrets.

Wake up and live. The more you do, the more joy, passion, life, and love you and this world will experience.

I know the path isn't easy. I've been failing down it for over ten years, now. But here is the secret. You won't ever arrive. You do your best, one step at a time, and as you do, you realize you are living, giving, and evolving. You realize your life, your gift, your journey is powerful, and beautiful.

I hope this book has given you a few steps. Most of all, I hope it has equipped and inspired you to be the best authentic, vulnerable, and amazing you that you can be.

You will still have tough days. You will put yourself out there, get super excited, and the world may go, "Eh."

So what. This isn't about the world. This is about evolving yourself. People are waiting to see if you are serious. People are waiting to see if you are committed...if your gift is the real thing. The more you dial into who you are and the more you consistently live your authenticity, the more you will attract action-takers and pull other winners into your circle.

A wise person once said what we expect when we start out is more than what is probable. But. What we can have after consistent action is way more than what we originally expected.

When you feel any challenge in giving your gift to the world—push through. Your gift is important. It can transform others.

Every journey starts with a step. Let's take it.

Jonathan Heston

FREEDOM HACKING CHEAT SHEET

(See Chapter 9 for the full exercise.)

1. Uncover the belief.

   Wait for the moment

   Follow the smoke trail

   List dump

1. Write down the belief statement.

2. Challenge the belief.

   Is this 100% true?

3. Change in and out of the belief.

   Who am I with this belief?

   Who am I without this belief?

4. Shift the belief.

   Do any of the alternative statements feel truer?

5. Evolve.

   What do I now want and how can I create that?

LEADING FEAR CHEAT SHEET

(See Chapter 10 for the full exercise.)

1. Feel the fear.

    Find the location in your body, rate from 1-10

2. Make the fear tangible.

    Ask yourself questions about the fear, so you can visualize it

3. Talk with the fear.

    Are you willing to communicate with me?

    What do you want?

    Are you trying to help me in some way?

    How are you trying to help me?

    Are you willing to help me without me feeling fear?

4. Make your power tangible.

    Ask yourself questions about your positive force, so you can visualize it

5. Fuse the forces.

    Ask the positive and negative forces to join

6. Test the results.

    Rate original fear

RECHARGE MEDITATION CHEAT SHEET

(See Chapter 12 for the full exercise.)

1. Giving and Gathering Breath

    Breathe in "pleasure", breathe out "energy"

2. Connecting

    Imagine warm light spreading from you to the world

3. Appreciation

    Think of things you appreciate in vivid detail

4. Trailblazing

    Imagine your future three years from now

5. Future Pacing

    Imagine taking steps today to help achieve the three-year vision

6. Receiving

    Ask and wait for insight from God

GIVING BACK

I spent over a year getting this book out. If you felt like you received value, it would mean the world to me if you invested thirty seconds to leave an amazon review.

I intend to leave this book as affordable as possible, so I can share the value with whoever wants it. But Amazon won't promote the book, unless readers (like you!) leave a quick review.

Regardless of your decision, thank you for your time with me. I'm honored to have shared this space with you.

EDGE WALKERS...

You don't have to go at this alone. I want to offer you a place in The Unlimited Self tribe.

Here are 13 reasons to join The Unlimited Self private Facebook group right now. (Touch Here to join on kindle, or go to https://www.facebook.com/groups/theunlimitedself)

1. The mission is simple. To create a community where you are supported in creating more freedom, love, and power in **every** area of your life. Where you can advance **your** world, whatever that may look like.

2. Radical Honestly. Nothing changes until there is a safe enough place where you can be *honest* with your frustrations, fears, pain, and the depth of your dreams. This community is full of Edge Walkers, striving to give their gift and live their life on the edge. We're authentic, vulnerable, and passionate. We constantly encourage, challenge, and share our journeys.

3. I know living life on the Edge isn't easy, but being connected with others pressing to their Edge massively ups your own chance of success. You know you're "the average of the 5 people you spend most of your time with." If you want to move *faster*...take responsibility to create what you want and surround yourself with likeminded men and women on the same mission as you.

4. Because of my commitment and our mission - ALL stages of growth are welcome if you're 100% committed to your expansion. Brand new to anything like this? Perfect. Personal growth junkie? Perfect. Run a multi-million-dollar business? Even better. Just starting on your entrepreneur journey? Awesome. You'll find things that will challenge and expand you

5. Are you stuck or stagnating? This group will help you get unstuck. I felt stuck for years, fighting the same battles, day in and day out. I finally realized I only have one life, and my life was too short to stay on that train ride. By watching others fighting and winning the same battles you are facing, it will help you demolish the feeling that you're alone *and* help you overcome what is keeping you from doing the same. Be inspired and freed—just by being around people on the same mission on you.

6. Living on your edge with others is a *blast*. Unlike work you want to put off, you'll *look forward* to involvement with this group. You'll discover it's the rawest, most real, and most authentic community online. No more feeling lonely.

7. You will get first dibs and access to anything I do. Such as events, special guides, masterminds, masterclasses...

8. Let's be honest. How many others in your life understand the depths of the *super human* feat you are trying to accomplish? The fears that you're facing. The burning desires that you carry. The deep pulling that you experience day after day? Don't let that fire in you be destroyed. Stoke it.

9. Communities like this were my secret tipping point, because I intentionally kept the inspiration in front of me and built a brand new network of friends, mentors, and supporters. I created The Unlimited Self, because I wanted to give **you** the same opportunity of mind-blowing paradigm shifts and life-changing friendships. I wanted a place where I was free to share my gifts with you – uncensored and undiluted.

10. I focus on helping you access your personal power (I already have a masterclass training available!) If you tapped into your true power, and lowered your internal negative emotional stress even a little bit, the results throughout your life would be tremendous. Trust me. Your loved ones will notice a difference. They deserve the real you. Not the "you" that's hidden under layers of negative beliefs and emotions.

11. You deserve to finally focus on yourself...right? When is the last time you focused on becoming a better you? Not better skills...but a better you? When you evolve *yourself*, everything around you will *level up*. This group is focused on you...are you?

12. You deserve a community that supports you and believes in you. But most importantly...who **calls you on your BS**. It's easy to find

cheerleaders that just want to get along. But you spend your life giving to others...who is giving to you? Who is taking the risk to help you see where you're playing small while still encouraging and loving you? Who is challenging you? Who is calling you on your BS...and believing in your greatness?

We only have one go at this life. Let's make the most of it. I know you can be the best vibrant you—the you hidden inside—all the time. Take a risk with me. The worst that can happen from joining is nothing. The best? You get upgrades t everything in your life at an incredible speed.

So join already. I have a free Masterclass in there already, but I'm not sure how long I'll keep it up. Don't wait around.

Go Here: **The Unlimited Self** (https://www.facebook.com/groups/theunlimitedself)

RECOMMENDED RESOURCES

Epic books:

The Prophet

The Big Leap

The Way of the Superior Man

The Dark Side of the Light Chasers

The War of Art

Love Without Conditions

Transcending The Levels of Consciousness

I Need Your Love, Is That True?

Outwitting The Devil

Conscious Loving

Radical Honesty

Choose Yourself

The Subtle Art of Not Giving a F*ck

Extreme Ownership

The Power of Now

Stealing Fire

Crazy Good

People you should know:

Christopher J. Stubbs

Dane Maxwell

Levi Darger

Austin Holt

Jesse Elder

Steve Chandler

Michael Hrostoski

Gay and Katie Hendricks

Dan Sullivan

ACKNOWLEDGMENTS

This book wouldn't have been possible without the amazing support of so many people throughout my life. But two people specifically helped a tremendous amount with this project, giving of their time and skill.

My wife, Chloe, blessed the project from the beginning (including a hefty investment we couldn't "afford"), gave priceless feedback and editing, and made this book visually awesome. I love you Chloe, and I'm beyond blessed that you are my dance partner in this glorious dance of life!

My mother, Dana Heston, who assisted tremendously with the first round of editing and feedback.

Several others contributed as encouragers, pushers, and thought provokers for this project. My brother, James Fry, who continued to push me to ship this, even months after I had it written, but still hadn't published. Everyone else who provided feedback and urged me to publish the book, including my dad - Johnny Heston and my grandfather - Ken Cobb.

Finally, I would like to express appreciation to the numerous people who have spoken into my life over the last 2 years.

First, my family of origins. Thank you for allowing me the gift of my own journey, even though it sometimes looked different and scary. Thanks for guiding and teaching me to think for myself, love unconditionally, live with integrity, and to push boundaries with wisdom.

To my mentor and coach: Christopher John Stubbs. I wrote this book before meeting him in person and have experienced unprecedented growth and transformation in my life over the last year because of meeting him. His impact on my life cannot be overstated. Love you, brother.

And countless other people who have spoken into my life including: Dane Maxwell and Jesse Elder.

ABOUT THE AUTHOR

First and foremost: I'm a husband, father, and man who is a lover of God.

Short version of my story: I pursued entrepreneurship for 17 years...stuck between failing miserably and being psychologically unemployable. I eventually hit such a wall of pain and frustration in life, I questioned everything. This lead to a process where I stopped trying to fulfill an equation for happiness and sourced my own happiness and power outside of anything external.

Through the help of a few amazing coaches, I realized I had abandoned myself. After facing the pain of reality, processing massive emotions, and learning to love and trust myself, I realigned with my purpose. My zone of genius is bringing breakthrough, feedback and guidance into the lives of others through powerful relationship. I finally experienced a deep sense of passion as I witnessed lives changing as I stepped into my gift.

Now my life is driven by a simple question: How good can I stand it and who can I serve? I've discovered how to be in a place of power and success, without being in a place of stress and overwhelm. I've said "no" to paths that seemed nice, but weren't me, and realigned my life around what I truly love and where I naturally create the most value for others.

My passion and skill is centered on supporting the personal freedom and power of men and women who advance the human race – especially entrepreneurs and business owners with families. Towards that end I've developed The Power Pyramid System, and In 2015, I teamed up with Christopher John Stubbs to assist driven achievers with creating epic marriages and living a life they love. I write, teach and speak, lead events and processes, lead online courses and webinars, and facilitate group events all around the U.S. to achieve this mission...but mostly, I create powerful one-on-one encounters. I am sought out for the transformational perspectives, strategies, and support one needs to ignite their life in a big way. I'm known for my ability to align big picture vision and strategic details with my client's unique individuality and approach. I don't believe one size fits all.

You'll often find me cuddling with Chloe, tickling Shiloh (my 4-year-old daughter), or laughing with Gideon (my 7-month son). I'm always learning and reading, enjoying Kansas City, writing and listening to music that moves me.

Thanks for being you, my dear reader.

To connect with me personally:
http://theunlimitedself.net/
jonathan@theinnerarena.com
facebook.com/jonathan.heston1
@jonathanheston

51958543R00140

Made in the USA
Lexington, KY
07 September 2019